GOD,
ARE YOU THERE?

KAY ARTHUR

HARVEST H

EUG

All Scripture quotations in this book are taken from the New American Standard Bible®, © 1960, 1962, 1963, 1968, 1971, 1972, 1973, 1975, 1977, 1995 by The Lockman Foundation. Used by permission. (www.Lockman.org)

Maps and charts in this book have been adapted from *The New Inductive Study Bible*, © 2000 by Precept Ministries International.

Cover by Koechel Peterson & Associates, Minneapolis, Minnesota

Cover photos © photos.com; Tom Henry / Koechel Peterson & Associates

GOD, ARE YOU THERE?
Copyright © 1994 by Kay Arthur
Published by Harvest House Publishers
Eugene, Oregon 97402
www.harvesthousepublishers.com

Library of Congress Cataloging-in-Publication Data

Arthur, Kay, 1933–
    God, are you there? : Do you care? Do you know about me? / Kay Arthur.
        p .cm.
    Includes the New American Standard text of the Gospel of John.
    ISBN-13: 978-0-7369-1828-2
    ISBN-10: 0-7369-1828-0
    1. Bible—Study and teaching. 2. Bible—Introductions. 3. Bible. N.T. John—Criticism, interpretation, etc. I. Bible. N.T. John. English. New American Standard. 2006. II. Title.
    BS600.2.A769   1994   94-6872
    220'8.07—dc20   CIP

Printed in the United States of America

08 09 10 11 12 13 /BP-KB/ 10 9 8 7 6 5 4

Contents

Finding the Answers to Your Questions

"God, what are You like?"

"Who are You?"

"Do You even exist?"

"Do You care about me?"

"God, do You even know about me?"

Have thoughts like these ever crossed your mind? Have you ever wondered who God is and what He is like? Or if He even exists?

If you have, don't dismiss these thoughts lightly. They are important. Just the fact that you have these thoughts means something. It means that God is drawing you to Himself—that He wants you to know the truth about Him.

How do I know that? Because I know God. And I want you to have an opportunity to know Him, too, and to find God's answers to your questions.

To find His answers to these questions, there is only one place to go. If you want to find the truth about God and what He says, you need to read the Bible.

How Can I Know for Sure the Truth About God?

People can tell you that God exists and that He knows about you and cares about you, but how do you know whether what you are hearing is true? Maybe it's just something they think is true, or maybe they simply "feel" it is true.

But what if their thoughts or their feelings are twisted or even wrong? After all, they are human beings, and all human beings don't think and feel the same way. Sometimes they are right, and sometimes they are wrong.

If human beings can be wrong, where can you go to find the truth about God—and be absolutely sure it is true? Only one place. In the one book that claims to be, and has been proven to be, the Word of God. The Bible.

Can God Give Purpose and Meaning to Your Life?

What if God can give purpose and meaning to your life even if you or someone else messed it up? What if He can show you how to live—no matter what your situation or circumstances? And what if He has promised to love and care for you and give you the wonderful gift of eternal life so that you can know for certain that the very moment you die you will find yourself in His presence to live with Him forever as His dear child?

Surely you would want to know how you can have that kind of relationship with God—a God who cares that much about you, whoever you are, wherever you are. Wouldn't you?

Well, my friend, that is what this book is all about. It's designed to help you know and understand the Bible so that you can see for yourself what it says about God, what it says about you, and what it says about becoming part of God's family.

Who Wrote the Bible?

The Bible is a book that claims to be different from every other book that has ever existed. It's different because it is the very Word of God, inspired by God. *Inspired* means that men wrote down exactly what God wanted them to write. The word *inspired* actually means "God-breathed."

In fact, let me quote what the Bible says about itself:

> All Scripture is inspired by God and <u>profitable</u> for teaching, for <u>reproof</u>, for <u>correction</u>, for <u>training in righ</u>-teousness; so that the man of God may be adequate [complete], equipped for every good work (2 Timothy 3:16-17).

In this verse God is telling us that the Bible came from Him and that it teaches us what to believe and how to live. (*Righteousness* means living the way God says we are to live.) The Bible also shows us where we are wrong (that is what *reproof* means). But it doesn't just leave us there!

The Bible tells us how to take what is wrong and make it right. What is wrong can be corrected, the Bible says, if we will listen to God and obey what He says! Isn't that encouraging? Plus, the Bible tells us how to live so that we can know how to handle every situation of life.

You know, just before Jesus Christ died on the cross for the sins of mankind, He prayed for everyone who would ever believe in Him. And in that prayer He asked that God would "sanctify" every believer. <u>Sanctify</u> means "<u>to set ap</u>art," so Jesus was asking that every believer would be set apart by God for God.

Then Jesus told us how God would set us apart. He said, "<u>Sanc</u>-tify them in the truth; Your word is truth" (John 17:17). Jesus said that God's Word is truth. Thus, when you know truth (the Bible) and live by what it says, you will be different from the rest of the world. Obeying God's truth sets you apart for God!

Therefore, my friend, you need to know what the Bible is and what it says. And to understand what it says, you need to know how to read it and study it for yourself. This book will help you learn how to do that.

You are going to be so excited about what you learn, but you have to remember that it is going to take some discipline on your part. Discipline is never easy, but in this case it is worth it, for it is a matter of life—life on the best level.

Now, on to the next logical question...

What Is the Bible?

The Bible, which claims to be the Word of God, is a book made up of 66 separate books. These 66 books were written by more than 40 men over a period of about 1400 to 1800 years. God inspired these men to write these books in a way that tells us exactly what He wants us to know and believe.

The Bible has two major parts. The first part is called the Old Testament, and the second part is called the New Testament.

The Old Testament

The Old Testament tells us how God created the world, how He created mankind, and how the first man and woman disobeyed Him. Eve chose to listen to Satan rather than God and ate of the forbidden fruit. Eve gave the fruit to Adam, who disobeyed God and ate of it also. As a result of this disobedience, mankind got into terrible trouble (God calls it *sin*). But because of His great love, God made a way for us to be restored—to once more be His friend and have a personal relationship with Him. The Old Testament tells us what He did to make that possible.

Most of the Old Testament centers around the history of the nation of Israel because that is the nation God chose to work through in a special way. Israel still exists today because of the promises God made to this nation way back then.

The Old Testament was originally written in two languages: Hebrew and Aramaic.* Most of it was written in Hebrew, the language spoken by the Jews, the people and nation especially chosen by God.

---

*Aramaic was a Semitic language closely related to Hebrew.

The Old Testament, which has 39 books, was written and completed almost 400 years before Jesus Christ was born. It was the only part of the Bible that existed until after Jesus died and arose from the dead. It was the Bible that Jesus knew and used while He was on earth because, of course, at that time the New Testament had not yet been written.

Although the Old Testament was originally written in Hebrew, it was later translated into Koine Greek. This language developed among the Greeks and was the language of Jesus' time. *Koine* means "common," and Koine Greek was the common language used in the world at that time (and until about A.D. 700). This translation, which was completed by about 100 B.C. (before Christ), was called the Septuagint. It was an important work because it allowed many more people to read and understand the Word of God in their language.

The New Testament

The New Testament was written after Jesus Christ died, arose from the dead, and then ascended into heaven. It was written originally in Koine Greek and is made up of 27 books.

The first four books of the New Testament are called the Gospels: the Gospel of Matthew, the Gospel of Mark, the Gospel of Luke, and the Gospel of John.

The word *gospel* means "good news." And the good news is that Jesus Christ loved you so much that He died to pay for your sins so that you could become part of God's family. Another important part of the good news is that Jesus Christ rose from the dead, never to die again. When you truly believe what the Bible says about Jesus Christ and decide to follow Him, to let Him be your Master, something miraculous happens. Your decision to walk with Jesus gives you a new life! It is an opportunity to start life over again as a new person, for God says that when you have this "new life" you become a "new creature." Because Jesus Christ lives in you through the Holy Spirit, He gives you the power to be different and to know that you will be raised from the dead to live with Him forever.

The Gospels tell us all about Jesus' life, His ministry, His death, and His resurrection. In fact, you and I are going to study one of the Gospels—the Gospel of John—in this book so that you can understand this good news for yourself and decide how you are going to live in the light of it.

Most of the rest of the New Testament is made up of letters, sometimes referred to as epistles, written to individuals or groups of believers in the early church. The epistles are filled with information about what we are to believe and how we are to live as children of God. You will discover this as you read and study them.

How Was the Bible Written and Preserved for Us?

As we mentioned earlier, the writers of the Bible, inspired by God, wrote down exactly what He wanted them to write. That original writing is called an *autograph*. Men called *scribes* then made copies of the autographs on scrolls of parchment (dried animal skins) or papyrus (a paperlike material made from the inner bark of a reed plant).

Although we don't have any of the original autographs, we have many handwritten copies of the originals. In fact, there are more copies of the original autographs of the Scriptures than of any other ancient writings that men accept as being authentic (real) and worthy of study.

Jewish scribes went through a special procedure to make sure nothing was left out, copied wrong, or added. If one error was found, the whole scroll was thrown away!

Why were they so careful? Because they were dealing with God's Word, and it was not to be changed or altered in any way.

Our all-powerful, all-wise God carefully guarded His Word so that not one word would be altered by man. Jesus Himself assured us of this when He said;

> Truly I say to you, until heaven and earth pass away, not the smallest letter or stroke shall pass away from the Law [Old Testament] until all is accomplished (Matthew 5:18).

Although the Bible is made up of 66 books written over 1400 to 1800 years, it fits together as one message with no contradictions in it. Why? Because it is God's Word.

Why Was the Bible Written?

The Bible was written so that anyone who wants to know who God is and how they are to live in a way that pleases Him can read it and find out.

God wants to bring us into a personal relationship with Himself. He wants to be a Father to us. In order to have that relationship, God has to talk to us. He has to explain who He is and how we can be brought into a close, wonderful relationship with Him. He also wants us to understand the blessings of living a life of obedience to His Word and the consequences of disobeying Him. He wants us to know the truth about life and what is going to happen in the future.

The Bible tells us everything we need to know about life. That, my friend, is why you need to study it for yourself.

How Is the Bible Organized?

The Bible is divided into two parts: The Old Testament comes first and is followed by the New Testament. At the front of each Bible you will find an index, which tells you the names of the 66 books of the Old and the New Testaments. It will also give you the page number where each book begins.

When you open a Bible, you will see that each book is divided into chapters, and each chapter is divided into verses. When the books of the Bible were first written, there were no chapter or verse divisions. These divisions were made many centuries later so that the Bible would be easier to read and study.

Having books divided into chapters and verses is also very helpful when you want to look for something specific. For example, when someone wants to tell you where to look in the Bible for a certain verse, he will record the name of the book, the chapter number, and the verse number. Thus, John 3:16 is a reference to the Gospel of John, the third chapter, the sixteenth verse. If you are to read more than one verse, it might look like this: John 3:16-36. In this instance, you are to read all the verses in chapter 3 from 16 through 36.

If someone is writing and quotes from the Bible, he or she will follow the quote with what we call its "address"—that is, the book, chapter, and verse where you will find it. So it will look like this:

> God so loved the world, that He gave His only begotten Son, that whoever believes in Him shall not perish, but have eternal life (John 3:16).

How Can You Find Out What the Bible Says?

To find out what the Bible says, you need to read it yourself in a way that will help you discover

- what it says
- what it means
- how you are to apply it to your life

Certain study skills will help you do this, and the best way to learn these skills is to do them! And that's what we're going to do together in the weeks ahead.

The study method we will use is called the *inductive* method. This is the very best way to study the Bible because it takes you directly to the Bible itself. It's a way to discover truth for yourself.

The inductive method doesn't tell you what the Bible means or what you should believe. Instead, it helps you understand and know the Bible by showing you how to see (observe) what it says for yourself. And after you see what it says, you can come to an understanding of what the author means.

As you study the Bible inductively, you should also read it devotionally. By devotionally I mean with a heart that wants to know God intimately and hear what God is saying to you. He speaks to us personally through His Word. Therefore, as you read, as you study, you also want to know God intimately and make sure that you take time to listen to what He is saying to you, to pause and say to God, "How do I live in the light of this?"

The Bible is a timeless book! Yes, it was written to others and about others, but God tells us that it was also written for us—to give us hope and to tell us how to live. It's for all people of all times, no matter what country or tribe they are from, no matter what their color, race, nationality, sex, age, or financial income.

When God speaks to "man," He is speaking to mankind—to women and men. In Jesus Christ, "there is neither Jew nor Greek, there is neither slave nor free man, there is neither male nor female; for you are all one in Christ Jesus" (Galatians 3:28).

In other words, God does not respect one race above another, one social status or caste above another, one sex above another. When we come to Jesus Christ, we are all the same. That is what God says. That is what God means. And that is the way it will be, because God is God.

Now, since the purpose of this book is to help you see for yourself what God says about Himself, about you, and about the relationship He wants to have with you, you and I are going to study the Gospel of John,* one of the books of the Bible. It is the fourth book of the New Testament.

When you finish this study, my friend, you will know for yourself what God says. Then you can decide whether you will believe Him or not.

How Are We Going to Study the Gospel of John?

We are going to study the Gospel of John one chapter at a time, and as we do, I will show you how to observe the Bible text in a way that will help you see for yourself what each chapter is teaching. I am not going to tell you what to believe. I will simply show you how to discover for yourself what God is saying. (That is why the chapters of *God, Are You There?* are titled according to the skill of Bible study you'll learn, rather than according to the subject of John—because we want you to discover the truths of each chapter for yourself.)

I'm asking you to commit to do seven weeks of this thirteen—week study. Once you get started, however, you will be amazed at how quickly the time passes and at how much you learn each week. And then if you continue, and I pray you do, you can finish the other six weeks of study. If you will do this study and believe what God says, your life will never be the same.

I will give you an assignment for five days of each week. If you cannot do your assignment every day, do the study at your own pace. Just remember that the Bible is truth, and if you want to know truth, you need to discipline yourself to study it. Also remember that there is one who does not want you to know truth. He is mentioned in John 8:44. Don't let him keep you from truth—finish your study!

---

* This book is often referred to simply as John.

You may find it very helpful to do this study with another person or in a small group and discuss it together. As you discuss what you have seen, however, always refer back to the chapter and verse you are studying. That way you can make sure your answers and insights are coming from the Bible rather than from what you or others think. At the end of this book, you will find a leader's guide that will help you week by week as you discuss what you learn and see how to apply it to your life.

Finally, you need to realize that you will not understand everything you read. You will understand what God wants you to understand. He will teach you a little bit, and when you understand that, He will teach you a little bit more. The more you continue to study His Word, the more you will see and understand. I have been a Christian for more than 40 years, and there is still much I have to learn. But how exciting that is! I can keep on learning more about my beloved Father and precious Lord and Savior until I see them face-to-face! I love it!

How Do You Begin Your Study?

Begin with Prayer

Prayer is simply talking with God. And because the Bible is God's book, you need to go to Him and ask Him to help you understand His book.

Just tell Him you want to see truth for yourself and that you would like Him to help you understand what He is saying.

Look for the Purpose of the Book

Every book in the Bible was written for a reason. So one of the first things you need to do when you read a book of the Bible is find the author's purpose for writing that book; or to put it another way, why God included this book in His Bible. If the author does not specifically tell you his purpose, then as you read look for what or who the author writes about most. This will help you discover the purpose of the book.

Sometimes you need to read a book through several times to see the author's purpose for writing. With the short books of the Bible that is not difficult, but with the longer books it can take some time.

However, finding the purpose is vital because the writer's purpose determines the way he lays out the material in the book, and it determines what he covers in his writing.

For example, the author's purpose or reason for writing the Gospel of John is given in John 20:30-31. The Gospel of John is printed in the back of this book beginning on page 151. Look for these verses and read them carefully. Then write out below why John wrote this Gospel:

Remember, everything John wrote in this Gospel was to help him accomplish this purpose. As you read each chapter, watch what he shares about Jesus Christ in order to achieve his purpose: to prove to you that Jesus is the Christ, the Son of God, so that you might believe in Him and thus have eternal life.

As you study each chapter, I will share some inductive study skills with you. Then, as you practice these skills, you will learn how you can study other books of the Bible inductively. And that is exciting, for you are not only going to learn the Gospel of John—you also are going to learn how to study the rest of the Bible! If you are a student, it will help you in your other studies too.

Week 1:

The Revealing "5 W's and an H" of Bible Study

Day One

1. At the end of this book you will find all of the Gospel of John printed out in a form called **Observation Worksheets.** This is the Bible text printed with space left beside it so you can make notes. This space is called the *margin.*

When you study the Bible inductively, you *observe* the passage you are studying. To observe something is to look at it very closely to see everything there is to see.

When you observe something carefully you see

a. what the whole thing looks like

b. what the different parts of it are like

c. how the parts relate to one another

A good way to observe a chapter of the Bible is to ask the **5 W'S and an H:** WHO, WHAT, WHEN, WHERE, WHY, and HOW.

For instance, when you read a chapter in John you should ask questions like these:

1. WHO is this chapter about or WHAT is this chapter about?

That God is the living God!!
And Jesus is the Christ, the Son of God!

It may be about a person—that's WHO.

OR

It may be about an event or some special subject—that's WHAT.

2. WHAT do I learn from this chapter about the person, event, or subject?

3. WHEN is this happening, or WHEN *will* it happen?

4. WHERE is this taking place, or WHERE *will* it take place?

5. WHY was this said? WHY was this mentioned? WHY did this person do this? WHY did this happen? WHY will this happen?

6. HOW was it done? HOW did it happen? Or, HOW *will* it happen?

You may not find answers to each of the 5 W's and an H in every text you study because they are not always there. When you observe the Word of God, you only need to see what God says. You do not need to read things into what He says—nor should you. If He wants you to know something, He will make it plain to you. He wants you to know truth and understand it.

He will tell you everything you need to know. You don't need to add anything to God's Word. As you carefully observe what He says, you will see truth and you will come to know Him as He really is.

You observe the text to discover what it says—that is **observation**.

In the process of observation, you'll discover what it means—that is **interpretation**.

Then, once you know what God says and what He means, you live in the light of it—that is **application**.

2. Turn to the Observation Worksheet for John 1 on page 151 of the appendix. (The appendix is the section at the back of the book, following Week 13, which contains extra materials you will need to do your study.)

Read through chapter 1 one time to see what it is about. (Remember to pray before you begin, asking God to help you.) When you finish, go to number 3.

3. What two people does this chapter talk about the most? Who are the main characters besides God? List them below.

a.

b.

That is enough for today. Tomorrow we'll start marking key words. You will be excited about what you learn. By the way, I'm so proud of you for making the effort to see truth for yourself. You will never regret it. God is going to open a whole new world to you, and you are going to be so grateful to Him.

Day Two

When you read a chapter of the Bible, you will find that certain important words are repeated a number of times. These are what we call **key words**. Like a key, they unlock the meaning of the Bible text.

You should mark each key word in a distinctive way so that you can spot it easily. Once you decide how to mark a key word, mark it in the same way each time it appears. You can use a color (which is best), a symbol, or a combination of the two to mark a key word.

For instance, I always color the word *believe* blue. I color the word *life* blue too, but I also use a symbol with this word—I put a box around it in green to distinguish it from *believe*. When I mark the word *devil* I just use a symbol—I use a pitchfork!

It will be helpful to list the key words which appear throughout the book you are studying on a piece of paper or a 3 x 5 card so you can use this as a bookmark. Then mark each word on the bookmark as you plan to mark it in the Gospel of John. You can use your bookmark as you go from chapter to chapter each week to remind you of how you are marking your words. I will tell you as we work through each week which words to add to your list, and even though they are on your bookmark I will remind you to continue to mark them as we go. (You won't always want to add every key word you mark because some key words are only in a particular chapter and you won't mark them after you finish your work in that chapter.)

1. Today you are going to read through John 1:1-18. As you read, you need to mark every occurrence of the key word *Word*. If you have colored pencils, you might color *Word* yellow each time it appears. If you do not have colored pencils, draw a diagram of an open book over it:

In the beginning was the Word, and…

2. Now read through John 1:1-18 again. This time you need to look for pronouns that refer to the key word. A *pronoun* is a word that takes the place of a noun. (Pronouns are words like *I, me, my, he, she, it, we, us, they, theirs*, and so on.) In John 1:1-18, these will be words such as *He, His, Him* which are used in the place of *Word* but refer to it. Color or mark these the same way you colored or marked the key word. Make sure the pronouns you mark refer to *Word* and not to someone else. I'll give you a clue! When you read the Bible text on your Observation Worksheet, you will begin to notice that all pronouns that refer to God the Father, Jesus Christ, or the Holy Spirit will begin with a capital letter.

3. Now that you have marked every occurrence of this key word in John 1:1-18 and every occurrence of the pronouns that refer to it, you need to mark any synonyms that refer to *Word*.

A *synonym* is a word that has the same meaning as another word or a word that refers to the same person, place, or thing. For instance, the words *God*, *Father*, and *Almighty* are all synonyms because they refer to the same person.

4. Now, lets do it. Watch for and mark the synonym(s) used in John 1:1-18 which refer to the *Word: life, light,* and *only begotten from the Father.*

Are you worried, my friend, that you are not getting the right answers? Don't worry! You are going to see truth for yourself. You are off to such a good start, and I am so proud of you. Remember, those who succeed are those who determine to keep on keeping on until they learn. I always tell my students, "Hangeth, thou, in there!"

By the way, the first week's lesson is a little long, but it's because chapter 1 is so long! Don't give up, though, because each week gets easier. Also, as you work through the weeks, you gain understanding and that makes it easier! Press on! Don't quit!

Day Three

1. After you mark the key words, make a list of what you observed from marking these words. (I'll show you how to do this a little bit later—so keep reading.) You can make your list in the margin of your Observation Worksheet. Or you can make a list on a piece of paper first and then copy it in the margin of your worksheet when you are happy with it.

Your assignment for today is to make a list of what you learn about the key word *Word*. So look at each place where you have marked *Word* or its pronouns and synonyms in John 1:1-18 and list what you learn from observing the text.

Do not put down anything that you have heard, think, feel, or believe—just put down what John 1:1-18 teaches you about the Word. (I am going to give you lots of room to make your list. You won't need all this space for your observations now, but you will need the space for an assignment you will do on Day Five.)

Now, let me get you started by showing you how to do the list. Note that I have put the verse number where I found what I saw as I listed it. I will give you the first two things that we see about the Word in this chapter:

The Word...

    v. 1. was in the beginning.

    v. 1. was with God.

    v. ___.

    v. ___.

2. Now then, my friend, did you write that the Word "is life" on your list? If not, look again at John 1:4 and see what it says. And in your list did you write "was the true Light"? Be sure you list all that you learned about the Word. If you think of something you didn't list, add that to your list.

3. Finally, let's think about your observations from John 1:1-18 and what they have to do with John's purpose in writing his Gospel.

Remember, John's reason for writing was that you, the reader, might see the signs Jesus performed and might believe that Jesus is the Christ, the Son of God, and that believing you might have life (John 20:30-31).

    a.   The first chapter of John doesn't tell us about signs Jesus did. But is there anything you observed in John 1:1-18 that points out that Jesus is the Son of God—or, to put it another way, that Jesus is God? List it below.

    b.   How is Jesus referred to in John 20:31? Can you see how what is said about Him in 20:31 is like what you see about Him in 1:1-18? Explain your answer.

Now, my friend, aren't you excited about what you have seen? Maybe you and a friend did this together, or maybe you did it with a teacher, and maybe you didn't see everything others saw, but think of the truth you discovered for yourself—*on your own!*

Day Four

1. In John 1:1-18 you read about someone besides Jesus Christ, the Word of God. Read John 1:6. What is this man's name? Write it out.

2. Read through John 1:1-18 and mark every reference to this man. Pick a color or a symbol. If you don't have colored pencils, you might want to use this symbol: John. (The marking is to show water—he is John the Baptist!)

3. Now, make a list of what you learned from marking each reference to this man. (Once again I am going to give you more space than you need at this point. You will use the space later.)

Day Five

1. Today you need to read through the rest of chapter 1. Read verses 19-51 and mark every reference to Jesus Christ in the same way you marked every reference to the Word. Don't forget to mark pronouns and synonyms. For instance, in John 1:29 you discover who the Word is—what His name is. Mark it like you marked *Word*. In John 1:29 Jesus is called the *Lamb of God*, therefore mark *Lamb of God* in the same way you marked *Word*. In verse 30 He is called a *Man*, so mark it like you marked *Word*.

2. Read through the same verses again and mark every reference to John, including any pronouns and synonyms. Use the color or symbol you used for him yesterday. (By the way, the John who is mentioned in verses 19-51 is not the same John who wrote this Gospel. Remember, in verses 19-51 this is John the Baptist.)

3. Now, faithful student, go back to the list you began on Day Three under number 1 (page 22) and add all that you learn from marking each reference to Jesus Christ in verses 19-51.

4. If you aren't too tired, write down all you learn about John on the list you began on Day Four, under number 3 (page 24).

5. Now, remembering John's purpose for writing this Gospel (John 20:30-31), look at your list about Jesus and at your list about John the Baptist and put a check mark by any truth that helps John accomplish his purpose in writing this book. Isn't it exciting to see from the very first chapter how much John tells us about Jesus Christ! In the remainder of his Gospel, John is going to show us these truths over and over, so watch for them.

6. In the appendix on page 217 you will find a chart called JOHN AT A GLANCE. This is a chart on which you can record the main theme of each chapter of the Gospel of John. The main theme is the most important subject or event covered in a chapter. It is the subject, the topic, that is talked about the most.

Taking time to figure out the theme and write it out helps you remember what that chapter is about. When you record the theme on the JOHN AT A GLANCE chart, you have an easy, handy way to find those truths or events without having to read through the book again if you want to refer to it. You have a summary of the events and truths of John at a glance!

Recording each chapter's theme also helps you see how the chapters relate to one another and to the author's reason for writing.

Record the theme of chapter 1 beside number 1 on the first line on the JOHN AT A GLANCE chart.

7. At this point, let's take a few minutes and see if you can apply anything you have observed to your life. To help you do this, let me give you some questions to think about carefully. It would be good to write out your answers; but if you are not comfortable doing that, just answer the questions in your heart.

John says that Jesus Christ is "the Lamb of God who takes away the sin of the world" (John 1:29).

When a person sins, he (meaning either he or she) runs his own life. He doesn't let Jesus be his Lord and Master, which means he does what he wants to do instead of what God tells him to do. He believes what he wants to believe even though it does not agree with what God says in His Word, the Bible. He doesn't believe Jesus is God, or if he does, he still won't honor Jesus as God and obey Him. When a person sins, he breaks or disobeys God's commandments.

a. Are you a sinner?

b. According to John 1:29, what will Jesus do with your sins?

c. According to John 1:12, how does a person become a child of God?

d. According to John 1:11, will everyone receive Jesus Christ?

This last answer is important to remember. As we continue our study, you are going to learn much about the people who refuse to believe that Jesus Christ is the Son of God and do not receive Him as their God and Savior. You will learn what will happen to them and how they will feel about you and respond to you if you believe in Jesus Christ. You will see what you are to do because of this and how you are to respond to them if you are a child of God.

8. Finally, here is one last question asked in two parts:

a. What is the most interesting or exciting thing you have learned about Jesus Christ from your study this week?

b. What disturbs you the most about what you saw? Or what is the biggest question you have?

You have just completed your first week of study, and it was a long one! I'm proud of you! My heart rejoices over your diligence! God will use what you are doing "to set you apart" in a very special way if you simply believe what He says and live like it. This is true "personhood"—being what God designed you to be.

Now until we meet again in two days, think about all you have learned from God's book, the Bible. "Live like Jesus," is what God says about His Son.

Week 2:

Discovering What's Happening— Putting Truth in Context

Day One

1. Read through John, chapter 2, on the Observation Worksheets in the appendix (page 154).

As you read this chapter, watch for and mark any references to time. WHEN something happens is important, so when God gives us "time indicators" we should pay attention to them. While He often doesn't mention a specific day, hour, or month, He does indicate time and the sequence of time in other ways.

For instance, in this chapter and throughout the Gospel of John you will read about Jesus going to certain feasts. Every Jewish male was required to go to Jerusalem three times a year to celebrate three annual feasts. Marking these feasts will help you see when something happened, because the feasts occurred at the same time every year.

When I study my Bible I always mark any *references to time* by drawing a clock in the margin. I also put an old-fashioned clock over words like *then, when,* and *after* if they show a progression of events, thus indicating a time sequence. If you do not want to use the clock symbol, color time references with one special color, such as green, or underline them with a pen.

You should also mark *references to locations*. For these you could use a double underline in a different color. For example, you would mark the location mentioned in John 2:1 like this:

> On the third day there was a wedding <u>in Cana of Galilee</u>, and the mother of Jesus was there.

When you see *the Passover* mentioned, mark it in the same way that you are marking time, since the Passover was a Jewish feast day celebrated at the same time every year. (Passover was a feast that began on the fourteenth day of the Jews' first month. That month was called *Nisan,* and it corresponds to either March or April of our calendar year. Remember this timing when you see Passover mentioned.)

These markings will help you see when and where Jesus went or when and where certain events happened. (Don't forget to add these references to time and location to your bookmark.)

2. When you finish reading John 2, go back to John 1 and color or underline the references to time and place in the same way you did in chapter 2.

Begin with John 1:1. What's the time phrase?

Now, beginning at John 1:28-43 watch for the phrase *the next day*. Mark it. It shows you what happened one day. Then keep watching for *the next day*.

3. Look at the time phrases you marked in John 1 and 2. Do you see the time sequence (the chronology) of events and how one event relates to another?

4. There is a map in the appendix (page 220) that shows the different places Jesus went. Look at the map so you can get an idea of where these things took place. This will put you into *context* geographically.

Context tells where something fits in relationship to other things.

1. Context can be geographical—the place where something happens in relationship to other places.

2. Context can be historical—the time in history where something fits with other events.

3. Context can be chronological—where something fits in time sequence with other events.

4. Context can be cultural—how something relates to the customs of the people of different lands and different times.

Context is one of the most important things to keep in mind as you study and interpret the Bible. The word *context* means "that which goes with the text." So if you are going to understand what something in the Bible means, you must always interpret it in its relationship to what is being said or written in the surrounding words, verses, chapters, and in the book itself.

Think of what you are learning! Jesus is a real person who lived at a specific time in history. You are learning about the land and the places where most of the events of the Bible take place. As you study other events of the Bible, think about how the good news about Jesus Christ came to your country.

Day Two

1. Read through John 2 again.

This time mark every occurrence of the words *sign* or *signs*. Choose a color for these words, and from now on whenever you see them in John color them the same way. Or, if you prefer, put a special diagram around these words, perhaps like this: ⬡. (Put *sign* or *signs* on your bookmark, because you want to mark it throughout John.)

Also mark the word *believed*. Pick a color! It is important to mark every occurrence of this word because the Gospel of John was written so that we might *believe* that Jesus is the Christ, the Son of God, and that *believing* we might have life in His name. Because of John's purpose for writing, *sign* (*signs*) and *believe* are key words in this book. Watch for every occurrence of *believe* in any of its forms. Look for and mark *believe, believed, believes, believing* as you work through the rest of this Gospel. (Also put all of these on your bookmark.)

2. Read through John 2 again—this time reading about one event at a time. As you do, you will see that these events change as Jesus moves from one place to another. In the left-hand margin of your Observation Worksheet, next to each event that occurs, write out as briefly as possible what happens when Jesus is in that particular place. For instance, opposite John 2:1-11 you would write "Wedding at Cana."

3. Now, turn to John 20:30-31 in your Observation Worksheets (page 213). Read these verses and mark the word *signs* the same way you marked it in John 2.

4. Look at verse 31 and mark the word *these* in the same way because this is a pronoun that is used to refer to the word *signs*.

Examine these verses and what they say about signs. Do this by asking the 5 W's and an H (WHO, WHAT, WHEN, WHERE, WHY, and HOW). Although you won't always find the answers to all of the 5 W's and an H, this process will help you learn a great deal and you'll better understand what God is teaching you.

To get you started, let me help you with John 20:30-31. I'll ask the questions and you write the answers.

a. WHO performs the signs?

b. WHERE were they performed—or WHO saw them?

c. WHERE were these signs written down?

d. HOW many of the signs were written down?

e. WHY were these signs written down?

5. Now go back to John 2 and answer the questions below. When you write the answers, record the number of the verses in John 2 that give you the answers.

a. WHAT is the first sign Jesus performed?

b. WHERE did He perform it?

c. WHO saw it, and WHAT happened as a result?

6. In the margin of John 2, next to the verses that mention the first sign Jesus did, write "Jesus' First Sign" and record what that sign was. Then look at the other places where you marked the words *sign* and *signs* and write in the margin what the sign either was or would be.

7. List what you learn in this chapter from marking *sign* and *signs*. WHO did the sign? WHAT was the sign? WHAT did the sign show? WHAT happened as a result? Write out your answers below. There's also room at the top of page 34.

Day Three

1. As you will see, John 3 is a very important chapter. Therefore read it very carefully. Ask God to help you understand what He is saying. Prayer is so important in studying the Word of God! God wants you to understand His book, and He promises that if you keep on asking and seeking He will answer.

When I tell you to talk to God—to pray—you may think, "But I'm not sure He even exists, or if He does, I'm not sure He would even listen to me." If this is what you are thinking, then, my friend, I want to say this—talk to Him and see what happens! If you are sincere, you will be wonderfully surprised.

2. Read through the whole third chapter of John just so you can become familiar with what is in this chapter. As you read, watch for a verse that tells you when Jesus goes to another place. Mark this in the same way you marked the instances in John 1 and 2 when Jesus moved from one place to another. You will see that John 3 covers two different events that happen in two different places. So draw your clocks and double-underline in green the geographical location (the place where something happens).

3. Now read John 3:1-21 and mark every occurrence of the two key words you marked the second day of this week's study: *believe* and *sign*. Remember to mark every form of the words. (Hint: In chapter 3 only *signs* is used, and *believe*, *believes*, and *believed*.) Mark these in the same way you did earlier.

4. As you read John 3:1-21, did you see any other important words repeated in these verses—words that helped you understand what's happening in these verses? Write them out below.

5. By the way, where do you think Jesus was when John 3 was happening? Look at John 2:23 and write out the answer to that question.

6. Where did Jesus go after that? Look at what you marked in John 3 and write out your answer.

Day Four

1. Today we are going to concentrate again on John 3:1-21. Read it through and mark the following key words: *born*, *born again*, and *eternal life*. Since these are all synonyms, mark them with the same color or symbol. After you finish you'll be able to spot where each one is used in John 3:1-21. (Add *eternal life* to your bookmark. And when you see the words *live*, *life*, and *life eternal* used in John, mark them like you mark *eternal life* because they are used as synonyms for *eternal life*.)

By the way, my friend, did you list these words yesterday when I asked you if you saw any other important words in this segment of John 3? You may have seen others, and that is good—but if you saw any of these, then you are already learning how to spot important words in a passage.

2. Now, let's look at John 3:1-21 and ask the 5 W's and an H to see what we can learn. Write the answers and put down the verses where you find them. Your answers do not have to be long.

    a. WHAT is John 3:1-21 about?

    b. WHO is Nicodemus? List everything you learn about him from this passage of Scripture.

    c. WHY did he come to Jesus?

    d. WHAT did Jesus tell Nicodemus he had to do in order to see the kingdom of God?

3. You marked every time the words *born, born again,* or *eternal life* were used in John 3:1-21. List on the next page everything these verses teach you about being born again. I'm going to leave you lots of space to write, but don't think you have to fill it up. (Some people write with bigger letters than others.)

4. You also marked the word *believe* and its forms yesterday.

    a. Read John 3:36 and mark *believes* in this verse.

    b. Now look at every place you marked *believe, believes, believed* in John 3:1-21 and look at verse 36 where you marked *believes*. Make a list of everything these verses say about believing.

5. Now, beloved student, think about all that you have seen today. What do you think about these things? How do you feel when you study them? Write out your answer. It helps to put it in writing.

Day Five

1. Remember the questions on the cover of this study book and the questions we asked at the beginning of this book? Does God exist? Does He know about you? Does He care about you? Can He help you?

Those are important questions, and God wants to answer them Himself. That's why He gave us His book, the Bible. He wanted all men, women, and children to be able to know truth because each of you, regardless of who you are, are precious to Almighty God. Therefore instead of going by what other people say or feel, you need to know what His Word says.

2. Read through John 3:1-21 and verse 36 again. Mark every reference to God like this: △ I don't often mark the references to God because it marks up my Bible too much. But I want you to see what you learn about God in this chapter. It's great!

As I said before, the use of a combination of colors or a color combined with a symbol for different words is very helpful in Bible study because colors are easier to distinguish than symbols. I use a triangle for God and color it yellow.

3. Now make a list of everything you learn about God from John 3:1-21 and from verse 36. Don't add your own thoughts, opinions, or feelings—which may be right or wrong. Rather, just record what the Bible says. God's Word is never wrong. It tells you what is truth.

As you look at each place where you marked "God," you know who the WHO is, so ask the other W's and an H. See what questions each of these references to God answers. Write down what you learn.

4. Now it's time to summarize in as few words as possible what John 2 and 3 are about. What is the main theme of each of these chapters? Remember, the *theme* is the most important subject or event covered in the chapter. Record the theme of John 2 and John 3 in the appropriate place on the JOHN AT A GLANCE chart (page 217).

There is so much more to see in John 3, so much more I would like to teach you! But I want to be careful not to give you too much to do at one time. I want you to stay with me.

5. So your last assignment today is to think about all you have learned this week from God's Word. What is God saying to you?

How can these truths be applied to your life today? Let's find out by answering several questions.

Nicodemus was told by Jesus that he could not enter the kingdom of God if he wasn't born again. Nicodemus was a religious man—a ruler of the Jews; yet his religion was not enough to give him eternal life, to get him into the kingdom of heaven. Nicodemus had to be born again of the Spirit.

a. Who or what do you worship, my friend?

b. Are you a Christian? Or do you have a religion without a personal, intimate relationship with God the Father? Deep in your heart do you know you can call Him "Father," knowing that you are truly His child, born of Him by His Spirit? How do you know?

c. If you are not a Christian but worship a different god, how does your god compare to what you have seen thus far in your study about God the Father and the Lord Jesus Christ? Make a list below and on the next page. Then compare the god you worship to your list.

What I've Seen About God and Jesus Christ in John 1–3

6. What did you see when you compared your list to the god you worship?

Now, dear one whom God loves just the way you are, if you desire to be born again, tell God and ask Him to help you understand all that being born again means. He will help you as you continue your study.

I am praying that you will finish what you begin, for I know finishing this study will make a *big* difference in your life. I also know that after you learn to study in this way, you can use these valuable study skills in every other study you do.

So persevere, Beloved. You'll never regret it. God's Word brings life, healing, and wisdom. It also connects you to God's power! (By the way, have you figured out by now, after studying John 3, why I call you "beloved"?)

Week 3:

Understanding Characters and Relationships

Day One

1. Read through John 4:1-42. As you read;

    a. Note WHERE Jesus goes and WHERE the events in these verses take place. Watch for and mark time phrases.

    b. Also mark the geographical locations in the same way you have in the previous chapters.

2. Write out in the margin the name of the city where the events of 4:1-42 happen.

3. Mark the following words in a distinctive way or color:

    a. *woman* (Also mark the pronouns that refer to her—like *she*. Don't add *woman* to your bookmark since it is a key word only in chapter 4.)

    b. *worship* (*worshiped, worshipers*)

    c. *life eternal* (Remember to mark this the same way you mark *eternal life, live,* or *life.*)

    d. *believe* (*believed*)

Day Two

1. Look up Samaria on the map in the appendix (page 220). Also note WHERE Jesus came from and WHERE He was going.

2. When you study the Bible, it's important to learn what you can from the text about people, people groups, and relationships. This is what life is about! God is concerned about people and about our relationships with them. Read John 4:9 and record what you learn about the Jews' relationship to the Samaritans.

It is believed that the Samaritans were a racially mixed people. When the Assyrians captured the Northern Kingdom of Israel in 722 B.C. they left the poorer and less-educated Jews in the land and took the other Jews to Assyria. They sent some people from other lands they ruled over to live in the city of Samaria. Some of the Jews who did not go into captivity married the people who came to live in their land. Their children were what some people call "half-breeds." Even their religious beliefs were often a blend of the differing beliefs of their parents. These people were called Samaritans, and the Jews didn't like them because they were a mixed race with a mixed religion.

3. Yesterday you marked *worship, worshiped,* and *worshipers*. On the following chart, list what you learned about the Samaritans' worship and the Jews' worship from marking these.

The Samaritans' Worship   *The Jews' Worship*

The Samaritans' Worship   The Jews' Worship

a. In John 4, WHO compares the Samaritans' worship to the Jews' worship and explains which is true worship? Can His word be trusted; is He right? (Read John 14:6 if you have any doubt.)

b. According to verse 22, WHERE is salvation from?

c. We saw in John 1:1-2 that Jesus is God and has been with God from the beginning. But we saw too that He was made flesh, that He became a man (1:14). To what nationality was Jesus born?

4. He was born a Jew. The Jews were "His own" who, according to John 1:11, did not receive Him for the most part. Maybe, my friend, you can relate to Jesus. Maybe your family or friends or people have rejected you, even persecuted you, because of your belief in God and His Son, Jesus Christ. If so, you know Jesus understands what you are going through.

    a. Read John 4:25 and write out WHO the Samaritans were looking for.

    b. According to John 4:26, HOW did Jesus respond to this?

    c. HOW did the woman respond to what Jesus said? Read John 4:29 and write out your answer.

    d. List below what you learned from marking *believe* and *believed* yesterday. Note WHO believes, WHAT they believe, and WHY they believe.

5. Just three last questions for today, my friend:

    a. Whom do you worship?

b. Where do you worship?

c. How do you worship?

Day Three

1. Read through John 4:1-42 again. Then ask God to show you truth so you might worship Him in truth.

As you read, make sure you have marked every reference to the *woman of Samaria*. Be sure to mark the pronouns (such as *she*) that refer to the woman in the same way. Also be sure to mark the word *woman*.

2. Make a list of everything you learned about the woman in the verses you marked.

3. What do you learn about Jesus' attitude toward women from this passage?

    a. Even though she was a Samaritan and an immoral woman, was this woman of importance to Jesus? How do you know?

    b. HOW did Jesus treat this woman?

    c. WHAT did He want for her?

    d. Were Jesus' disciples surprised that He talked with this woman?

    e. What might this tell you about how women were treated at that time?

    f. Was it God's will for Jesus to treat the Samaritan woman the way He did? How do you know this from the text?

    g. According to the text, WHAT was Jesus' food?

4. What is the attitude toward women in your religion, in your country, in your society? What do the people you know think about the birth of girls and about women in general? How are they treated? Would they kill a woman for being immoral and let the

man go free? What do you think about women and why? Write it
out and then compare it with what you saw in Jesus.

5. Read John 4:43-54.

    a. Note where Jesus goes next and mark it the same way
       you have been marking geographical locations.

    b. Mark the words *sign* (*signs*) and *believe* (*believed*).

    c. List below who believes and why.

Day Four

1. Read through John 5 and mark the following key words:
Father, *live* (*life*), *testify* (*testifies*, *testified*), *testimony*, and *believe*
(*believes*, *believed*). If you have marked any of these words before,
mark them in the same way you did in the other chapters and on
your bookmark.

As I told you earlier, I mark any reference to God the Father
with a triangle and color it yellow. (Note: Be careful when you
mark pronouns that refer to the Father because it is easy to get
confused and mark ones that are referring to the Son! Just think
carefully and you will do fine!) Remember, I colored *life* blue since

life comes from believing, but then I boxed it in with green so I could distinguish *believe* from *life*.

2. Look back through chapter 5 and see if you need to mark time phrases or geographical locations. If you do mark any locations, check the map in the appendix to find where they are.

Day Five

1. Read through John 5:5-47 and mark every reference to *Jesus*, including pronouns and synonyms such as *Son*. I mark references to Jesus like this: ⟍ and I color the symbol yellow. Remember, a synonym is another word that means the same thing or refers to the same person, place, or thing. You will see a different synonym used for Jesus in these verses. It is *Sir*. Be sure not to miss it! Also, although I have you mark "Jesus" in this chapter, I do not always mark every reference to Him in other chapters because too many marks can get confusing. We are marking all the references in this chapter so you can see the Son's relationship to the Father.

2. Now list below what you learn about God the Father and about God the Son.

God the Father   *God the Son*

3. Now, Beloved, take a few minutes to think about the relationship between the Father and the Son. Remember, in John 1:18 you saw that Jesus came to explain the Father to us.

    a. According to John 5, WHAT does Jesus do that explains the Father to us?

    b. How should we live if we want to explain God the Father and God the Son to people?

4. List below what you learn from marking the words *life* and *live* in this chapter.

5. Think again about John's purpose for writing this Gospel (John 20:30-31) and how what he writes in this chapter helps him achieve his purpose. Write it out.

6. My friend, from what you have seen in John 4 and 5, do you think Jesus knows that people exist? Do you think He cares about them? What did you learn this week about people and relationships?

7. Now, do you think God cares about you no matter who you are, whether you're a man or a woman? And what about your race, nationality, status, religion? If you were to believe what you have studied in the Gospel of John, how would you know?

8. Finally, record the main themes of John 4 and 5 on the JOHN AT A GLANCE chart (page 217).

Week 4:

Eat My Flesh, Drink My Blood—Is It Figurative or Literal?

Day One

1. Read through John 6 (page 166).

2. Mark every reference to *bread* along with all its synonyms (*loaves, food, manna, bread out of heaven*) and pronouns (*it*). Mark all these the same way because basically they are used to point to the same thing—the bread of life. You might want to mark it like this ⌂ and color it light brown. (Don't add *bread* to your bookmark since it is a key word only in this chapter.)

3. Also mark every reference to geographical locations as you have done since observing John 1. Consult the map in the appendix (page 220) so you know where things are occurring.

4. John 6 also mentions "Passover, the feast of the Jews." As you read through John you will find many references to various feasts that Jesus attends. For a better understanding of the importance and meaning of these feasts, consult THE FEASTS OF ISRAEL chart in the appendix (pages 218-219). You might want to study it after you do your work for this week.

Also you might want to mark every reference to the feasts in a special way. (Remember, you are marking Passover as a time indicator already.) I write the names of the feasts in the wide margin of my Bible so that I can see quickly whenever a chapter mentions a feast. (The chart will tell you when the feast occurs.)

Day Two

1. Read through John 6 again today. When you are studying the Bible it is good to read chapters over and over again. As a matter of fact, it is good to read through the whole book you are studying over and over again so you keep the big picture before you. Reading through the entire book helps you keep everything in the book in context. Remember, context is that which goes with the text, and when it comes to correctly understanding what verses mean, context must rule. God never contradicts Himself, so Scripture never contradicts Scripture.

Yesterday when you read through John 6 you marked the word *bread* and its synonyms. *Bread* is a key word only in this particular chapter. As I explained earlier, sometimes key words are used throughout an entire book and help you see the main theme of the book. Other times they are used only in certain chapters or segments of the book.

Today you are to mark the following key words:

 a. *life (eternal life)*. Also, mark *live* in the same way if it refers to eternal life.

 b. *believe (believed, believes)*

 c. *My flesh, His flesh*. Mark this the same way you marked *bread*. Look at John 6:51 so you can see why you are to mark it this way.

 d. *sign (signs)*

2. Make a list of what you learn from marking the word *sign* (*signs*). Record your list on the Observation Worksheet if you have time.

Day Three

1. Read through John 6:1-40 again. This time watch HOW Jesus uses the sign of the loaves and fishes to teach the crowds. WHAT does He want them to see? Write it out.

2. List everything you learn about the true bread that comes down from heaven.

3. List below everything you learn from marking *life* and its synonyms in John 6.

Day Four

1. Read John 6:39-59. Mark every reference to *raise it* or *raise him on the last day*. Then list what you learn about who is going to be raised up on the last day.

2. In John 6:51-58 when Jesus talks about eating His flesh and drinking His blood, do you think He is speaking figuratively (symbolically) or literally (actually)? Why? What do you think He means? What is the point He is trying to make? Think about the whole context of this chapter.

3. When Jesus talks about being raised up on the last day, is there any implication of reincarnation in His teaching? Is He talking about being brought back in another form—say that of an animal—or being brought back at a different level of attainment?

Think about what you listed in number 1, then look up John 5:24-29. Now write out your answer according to what you have seen in the Gospel of John so far. (By the time you get to the end of your study of the Gospel of John, you will have even greater insights into what happens to a born-again Christian when he or she dies.)

Day Five

1. Read John 6:60-71. Mark any reference to *Spirit*. I usually mark it like this: Spirit (I use one side of the triangle that I use to symbolize God the Father for my "Spirit" symbol and then color it yellow.)

2. HOW did the disciples respond to what Jesus was saying in this chapter? WHY?

3. HOW did the twelve respond?

4. How do you feel about what Jesus is saying about eternal life in this chapter? If He is speaking truth (and He is), what does this tell you about *your* future? Why?

5. Read John 6:64-71 and note or mark every reference to Judas. Judas was chosen by Jesus to be one of the 12 disciples who would go everywhere with Him. WHAT do you learn from these verses about Judas? List your insights below.

6. If Judas could betray Jesus, then could others who professed to be His disciples do the same? Or to put it another way, do you think all who *say* they are Christians are really true Christians just because they *say* they are? How would you know?

7. Beloved, from all that you have seen, according to the Word of God, is it possible to have eternal life apart from Jesus Christ?

8. Do not forget to record the theme of John 6 on the JOHN AT A GLANCE chart.

Well, my friend, you have completed four weeks of study, and I am so very proud of you. I wonder if you realize all that is taking place as a result of your study. You are not only learning how to study, not only developing and strengthening your reading and understanding skills, but you are also interacting with Truth, with God! These are the very words of God! What a privilege it is to discover truth for yourself. These are words of life! Beloved, live by them!

Week 5:

Contrasts and Comparisons—Did You Get the Point?

Day One

Read the entire assignment for the day, faithful student, before you begin any part of it.

1. Read John 7 (page 171). As you read, carefully note WHAT is happening, WHERE it is happening, and WHEN it is happening. Don't forget to look for and mark locations and references to time as you read. (Remember to mark the feasts because they help you see time.)

Now, write out your insights below.

    a.   WHAT is happening in John 7?

    b.   WHERE is it happening?

    c.   WHEN is it happening?

2. As you read through John 7 again, mark the following key words with their synonyms and pronouns: *feast, believed (believes, believing), signs.*

3. Also mark the key words, *the Christ.* Mark this synonym for Jesus in a special way. Make an exception this time, however, and do not mark other synonyms, because all I want you to see in this chapter is the use of the term "the Christ." (By the way, *Christ* is another word for *Messiah*—Remember John 1:41?—and refers to the one God promised to send who would deliver the Jews and reign as their King.)

Day Two

1. Today, read through John 7 paragraph by paragraph. You can tell when a paragraph begins because the verse number is in darker type than the numbers of other verses. Remember, a paragraph is several sentences that are grouped together because they have something in common, such as a certain thought or event.

As you finish each paragraph, summarize in a sentence or two what happens in each paragraph. Watch the timing in each paragraph. (By the way, the feast that Jesus goes to in John 7 is the Feast of Tabernacles, or Booths.)

Here are the paragraph divisions. Write your summary of the event or teaching beside each one:

    a. John 7:1-9

    b. John 7:10-13

c. John 7:14-24

d. John 7:25-36

e. John 7:37-44 (Also mark the word *Spirit* and list what you learn about the Spirit in this passage.)

f. John 7:45-53

2. Now list everything you learned from marking *the Christ* yesterday.

3. WHO were Jesus' enemies? WHO hated Him and wanted to seize and kill Him? What do you learn from this? Is everyone going to love Jesus—or those who belong to Him? What will some people do to them?

4. Are you thirsty, my friend? Have you not yet found that which satisfies the deep emptiness and longing within? Has your religion really satisfied you? Have you ever considered coming to Jesus—even if it means persecution or death?

5. What do John 6:37,39,44, and 54 promise you?

Think about all this, Beloved, and talk to God about it. Surely you have seen by now that if the Bible is the true Word of God, God does know about you and He does care. If He didn't, He surely wouldn't have given His only begotten Son to die for you so that you would not perish but would have eternal life (John 3:16).

Day Three

1. Read John 8, and in a distinctive way mark every occurrence of the word *sin* (*sins*). (Be sure to add this word to your bookmark.)

2. Now list everything you learn about *sin* from John 8. You may want to copy this list in the margin of your Observation Worksheet when you complete it.

3. Read through the chapter again and look for time indicators and locations. Mark these in the same way you have in John 1–7.

Day Four

1. Read John 8:1-11.

   a. In several sentences summarize what this paragraph is about.

   b. Leviticus 20:10-16 gives the law regarding sexual sins. The text is printed out below. Read it carefully and note the various types of immorality (sexual misconduct) to which it refers, as well as the penalty for each.

   If there is a man who commits adultery with another man's wife, one who commits adultery with his friend's wife, the adulterer and the adulteress shall surely be put to death. If there is a man who lies with his father's wife, he has uncovered his father's nakedness; both of them shall surely be put to death, their bloodguiltiness is upon them. If there is a man who lies with his daughter-in-law, both of them shall surely be put to death; they have committed incest, their bloodguiltiness is upon them. If there is a man who lies with a male as those who lie with a woman, both of them have committed a detestable act; they shall surely be put to death. Their

bloodguiltiness is upon them. If there is a man who mar-
ries a woman and her mother, it is immorality; both he
and they shall be burned with fire, so that there will be
no immorality in your midst. If there is a man who lies
with an animal, he shall surely be put to death; you shall
also kill the animal. If there is a woman who approaches
any animal to mate with it, you shall kill the woman
and the animal; they shall surely be put to death. Their
bloodguiltiness is upon them (Leviticus 20:10-16).

According to what you see in Leviticus 20:10-16, why
do you think the men brought this woman who was
committing adultery to Jesus?

c. How many does it take to commit adultery? (Adultery
is having a sexual relationship with a person you are not
married to. Regardless of what your culture says, it is a
sin in God's eyes.) Where was the man? What does this
show you regarding the hearts and intents of these men?

d. HOW did Jesus handle the men? WHAT did He want
them to see?

    e. HOW did Jesus respond to the woman? Did He approve of her actions? Did He think she hadn't sinned?

    f. Are you living a sexually pure life, or are you guilty of breaking God's law as recorded in Leviticus 20? In light of what you've learned about sin from marking the word throughout John 8, what would Jesus tell you or anyone who is living immorally by breaking His law?

2. Read John 8:12-32 and mark the key words you have been marking throughout the Gospel of John if they are used in these verses. Also mark the words *true* and *truth*. Then make a list of everything that is *true* or *truth*. Record this list in the margin of your Observation Worksheet too. (Put *true* and *truth* on your bookmark.)

3. When you observe the text, it is important not only to mark key words, geographical locations, and references to time, it is also important to watch for **contrasts** and **comparisons**. Contrasts and comparisons often help the reader see in a deeper, vivid, or more picturesque way what the author wants his readers to understand. Therefore, when you study the Bible, watch for contrasts and comparisons.

a. A *comparison* shows how things are alike or similar to one another. Many times when the author wants to compare something he will use the words *like*, *as*, *as it were*. Look at John 8:12. WHAT does Jesus compare Himself to in this passage?

b. A *contrast* is a comparison of things that are different or opposite, such as sons of night and sons of the day, or proud versus humble. Look again at John 8:12. WHAT is contrasted in this verse in respect to those who follow Him? Write it out.

4. Now read John 8:21-23. To WHOM is Jesus speaking? WHAT does He contrast in these verses? Write out the contrasts below.

Day Five

1. According to John 8:24, WHY would the Jews die in their sins? WHAT did they have to believe?

2. Did you notice that the word *He* in John 8:24 is in italics? When you see any words in the Bible text in italics, you can know these were added by the translators to make the text easier to understand. So when the New Testament was translated from Koine Greek to English, the word *He* was added.

When Jesus said to the Jews, "Unless you believe that I am," the Jews asked Him who He was. They asked because Jesus had just claimed to be God by using the same name that God gave Moses to describe Himself. It was "I AM." Let me write out Exodus 3:13-15 for you so you can see it for yourself. As you read, note that "I AM" in Exodus 3:14 is God's memorial-name to all generations.

> Moses said to God, "Behold, I am going to the sons of Israel, and I will say to them, 'The God of your fathers has sent me to you.' Now they may say to me, 'What is His name?' What shall I say to them?"
>
> God said to Moses, "I AM WHO I AM"; and He said, "Thus you shall say to the sons of Israel, 'I AM has sent me to you.'"
>
> God, furthermore, said to Moses, "Thus you shall say to the sons of Israel, 'The LORD, the God of your fathers, the God of Abraham, the God of Isaac, and the God of Jacob, has sent me to you.' This is My name forever, and this is my memorial-name to all generations."

3. When we speak of the *deity* of Jesus Christ, we are saying Jesus Christ is God, one with God the Father, equal to Him in character and attributes.

> a. Look at John 1:1-2,14. How do these verses show the deity of Jesus Christ?

b. The Gospel of John stresses the fact that Jesus Christ is God—not *a* god, but God in the flesh. So as you study John, watch for any other verses that show Jesus is one with the Father or that Jesus Christ is God.

c. There are two other places in John 8 where Jesus refers to Himself as I AM. Look these up and write down what you learn.

1) John 8:28

2) John 8:58-59

The Jews could stone someone for blasphemy. If they didn't believe Jesus was God when He was claiming to be God, they would consider it blasphemy. This truth is seen in John 10:33, which we will look at later.

4. According to John 8:31-32, WHAT do true disciples of Jesus do? WHAT does truth do? Where do you think truth is found?

5. WHAT is contrasted in John 8:32-36?

6. In John 8:37-47, two fathers are contrasted. List what you learn about these fathers and about those who belong to them.

God the Father   *The Devil*

7. From what you have just observed in God's Word, who would you say is your father, and why?

8. Although Jesus Christ is God, what kind of relationship did He have with the Father? Read through John 8:26-59 and list below everything you observe in these verses in regard to Jesus' relationship to the Father.

In other words, what God is like, Jesus is like. What God can do, Jesus can do. This is true because they have the same nature—the nature of God! Jesus also took on the nature of man, but He never ceased to be God. So Jesus holds a unique position—He is the God-man.

Now, think about what you have written. What you see Jesus demonstrating is the way you and I ought to live in relationship to God the Father.

9. Now, Beloved, I must leave you with a few vital questions.

   a. Do you believe that Jesus Christ is God? If your answer is "No," then what will happen to you, according to God's Word in John 8:24?

   b. And what about anyone who would tell you Jesus Christ is not God, or that He is just *a* god like you or anyone else could be? What about those people? What will happen to them according to John 8:24? Even if they are nice? Sincere? Or even if they believe Jesus was a good man, a prophet?

   c. Are Jesus' words true? What did He say? Are you going to believe Jesus or man?

   d. If a man doesn't believe Jesus Christ and is not born again, then who is his father? And what is his father like? Look at John 8:44.

10. Record the themes of John 7 and 8 on the JOHN AT A GLANCE chart in the appendix (page 217).

Oh, Beloved, look at all you have learned just by studying God's Word for yourself. According to John 6:63, the words Jesus has spoken to us "are spirit and are life." Don't quit studying them. You may have committed to do this study for seven weeks. If so, in two weeks you will have fulfilled your commitment. You are to be commended. But may I urge you to continue? There are seven more lessons after next week, and if you complete them then you will have a good grasp of the whole Gospel of John. Truly the best is yet to come. In chapters 13–17 you are going to learn all about the abundant life that belongs to those who have believed that Jesus is the Christ, the Son of God, and in believing have life in His name.

May I urge you—plead with you—not to stop studying, for I know what other encouraging and life-transforming truths are still to be discovered. I know how they have blessed multitudes, and I don't want you to miss that blessing, my friend.

Week 6:
What's the Occasion?
What's the Lesson?

Day One

Read John 9 (page 179). As you read this chapter, watch for key repeated words and mark them. Also watch for and mark time indicators and locations.

1. List the key words below.

2. Now answer some of the 5 W's and an H:

   a. WHAT is John 9 about?

   b. WHO are the main characters in this chapter? List them.

    c. WHERE does it take place? (If you can't find the answer in chapter 9, then go back to the end of chapter 8.)

    d. WHEN does all this happen? What day of the week?

Day Two

1. Read through John 9 again. If you did not mark the following key words, mark each in a special way so you can easily spot where the word is used in the chapter: *signs, sin (sins, sinned, sinner), blind, believe, see (sees, seeing, seen, sight).*

I marked each occurrence of the word *see* and its synonyms with two eyes: see. Then I colored them yellow to represent the fact that they could now see. I marked *blind* the same way, but colored it brown because they could not see. I am just sharing this so you can get ideas on how to mark words. Sometimes it helps to see what others do!

2. List below and on the next page what you learn about the main characters in John 9.

Jesus   *The Blind Man*   *His Parents*   *The Jews*

Jesus	*The Blind Man*	*His Parents*	*The Jews*

3. Now look at the key words you marked. If you have time, take a sheet of paper and list everything you learn from marking each of the words. As you look at each occurrence of each word, ask the 5 W's and an H. (At times you may find an answer to only one of the 5 W's and an H.)

When you take the time to make lists, you usually see new insights from the text that you missed when you simply read through it. Also, this gives you time to think about what God's Word says and how it applies to your life.

You may want to record your lists on your Observation Worksheets as well.

Day Three

John 10 is such a wonderful chapter. I know it will be a blessing to your life, Beloved.

1. Read through the chapter and mark every reference to *sheep.* Make sure you mark each pronoun that refers to sheep, such as *them* or *they.* Also, be sure to mark *flock* in the same way.

2. Watch for the word *blind* and mark it like you did in chapter 9.

Day Four

1. Read John 10 again. Watch for time indicators and locations and mark these. Also mark the following key words and their pronouns: *Shepherd* (the pronouns would be *My, I, Me, Him, His, He*), *the Jews, believe (believed), sign, the door, the thief*, and *the Christ.*

Although both synonyms refer to Jesus, don't mark *the Christ* in the same way you marked *Shepherd.* And remember that *the Christ* refers to the Messiah whose coming was promised in the Old Testament—the One who would save and deliver the Jews. Remember, too, John was writing because he wanted others to know and believe that Jesus was the Christ. So I want you to mark *the Christ* in a special way so you can quickly see how it is used. Mark it as you did before in chapter 7.

2. Now that you have marked the key words, make a list of everything you learn about the Shepherd and about the sheep.

The Shepherd   *The Sheep*

3. Since you also marked every reference to the thief, let's see what we can learn about the thief.

    a. WHO is the thief contrasted with? List the ways they differ.

    b. If Jesus is the Shepherd, who do you think the thief represents? If you do not know the answer, you may want to go back to John 8:44 and find any similarities between the one mentioned in John 8:44 and the thief. Write out your answer.

Day Five

1. When you read a chapter that contains a particular teaching, such as John 10 does on the sheep and the Shepherd, *it is always good to find out what caused or prompted the teaching.* So think about what just happened in John 9 and how it relates to the teaching in chapter 10. Also remember what you saw when you marked the word *blind* in chapter 10, since Jesus and those around Him were still discussing what happened in John 9. Now: What was the occasion? Jesus is a master teacher, and as such He uses situations as occasions for teaching valuable lessons for our lives.

    a. Were the Pharisees (Jews) wanting to go to heaven?

    b. Were they willing to go through "the door" (Jesus)?

    c. WHAT did the Jews accuse Jesus of in John 10:33?

    d. Were the Jews "blind" to who Jesus was? Therefore, were they sheep and in His sheepfold?

Of course, the Jews were not willing to come to God through Jesus, the door to the sheepfold. So Jesus taught about sheep and a shepherd.

2. Review John 20:30-31, which gives John's reason for writing this Gospel.

    a. How do John 9 and 10 help John accomplish his purpose in writing his Gospel?

    b. Just in case you missed it, read John 10:30-39 again. How do these verses show the deity of Jesus Christ (the fact that Jesus is God, one with the Father in character and attributes such as holiness, righteousness, mercy, and love)?

3. When you study your Bible, it is good to write down cross-references in the margin. A *cross-reference* is the book, chapter, and verse of another place in the Bible that either says basically the same thing that you are studying or is a reference that helps you understand more clearly what you are studying.

Because the deity of Jesus Christ is so important, it is good to set up a system of cross-references that point to other places in the Bible where this teaching is mentioned.

For example, if you wanted to cross-reference *deity* in the Gospel of John, you would write DEITY in the margin of your Bible next to John 1:1. Under it put the next reference in John that specifically shows that Jesus is God. Therefore, next to John 1:1 you would write

DEITY
John 1:14

Then you would go to John 1:14 and in the margin you would write DEITY. Under it put the next reference to the deity of Christ, which is John 8:24. Next to John 8:24 write DEITY and put John 8:58; then next to John 8:58 write DEITY and put John 10:30-33.

4. Review what you observed and listed about the sheep and the Shepherd yesterday.

5. At the end of this lesson there is a section called INSIGHTS ON SHEEP. You will enjoy reading these insights! They are fascinating—a description of what many people are like! They will help you appreciate what Jesus says in John 10. (Remember, the Jews of Jesus' day were far more familiar with sheep than many of us are today.)

After you read INSIGHTS ON SHEEP, make a list of the ways you relate to what you just learned. How are you like a sheep?

6. According to what you have learned from John 10,

    a. WHAT is the only way to get into God's sheepfold?

    b. WHAT will happen to God's sheep?

    c. Is Jesus Christ your shepherd, or would you like to have Him as your shepherd? Would you like to be His sheep? Why or why not?

    d. Write a prayer to God and tell Him what is on your heart and how you feel about what you just learned from His message in John 9 and 10.

7. Record the themes for John 9 and 10 on the JOHN AT A GLANCE chart.

8. Now, Beloved, learn to watch the "occasions" in your life and ask God what He wants you to learn from them when they happen. Remember, He's there with truth to get you through every incident. He cares!

Insights on Sheep

1. The life of a sheep depends a lot on what kind of shepherd it has. If the sheep has a mean or cruel shepherd, it would probably suffer and its life would be hard. Or if the shepherd were lazy and didn't take care of the sheep, it might be hungry or even starve!

 But if the shepherd was gentle and brave and didn't think of himself first, then the sheep would grow to be healthy, strong, content, and happy.

2. More than any other kind of animal, sheep need attention and care. The shepherd must protect the sheep from cougars, wolves, dogs, and thieves. The shepherd must protect his sheep *at all times* of the day and night. (And you know, God is your Shepherd, and He protects you all the time too!)

3. Sheep are timid and fearful animals. They get scared very easily, and this fear keeps them from doing many things that are good for them.

4. Sheep are "mass-minded"—they have "mob instincts"—they will all do what every other sheep is doing! If one sheep gets scared and runs, all the others will run with it, whether or not they know why they are running.

5. Sheep are animals of habit. They like to keep following the same trails over and over. They will keep grazing on the same land until they practically ruin the land—and they will eat bad grass!

6. Sheep are also known to be very stubborn animals. They need the shepherd to guide them around.

7. Sheep are very stupid, dumb animals. They will sometimes just freeze if there is danger around. Sometimes they won't even try to run to safety; they will panic and not even cry out.

8. It's easy to tell who owns the sheep because each shepherd gives his sheep an earmark. The earmark is like a brand mark. The shepherd cuts a certain mark into each one of the sheep's ears. And each shepherd gives all his sheep the same earmark.

9. Sheep will not lie down and rest unless they

    a. are not afraid

    b. get along with all the other sheep

    c. do not have any flies or pests bothering them

    d. are not hungry

10. Sheep will butt each other with their heads. They also have a "butting order." The oldest sheep usually has the highest position of power. If a younger sheep is eating in a patch of grass the oldest one wants, he will butt the younger one out of the way! The younger ones will act just the same way to sheep younger then themselves. *But* when the shepherd comes around, the sheep forget what they were fighting over, and they stop and behave themselves.

11. A sheep has to have good land to feed on or it will stay hungry! If a sheep is hungry, it will stay on its feet and constantly be searching for food to satisfy its hunger. Sheep cannot sleep if they are hungry, and they are not much good to the owner if they stay in that condition. They get nervous and upset very easily, and if they don't eat the right food, all sorts of things will bother them.

12. Sheep are bothered by many different pests—all kinds of flies, mosquitoes, gnats, and other flying insects. Many of these insects will aim straight for the nose of the sheep! If they get in the sheep's nose, they may lay eggs. When the eggs hatch, the larvae will get into the passages of the nose and cause swelling and irritations and sometimes blindness. The sheep will beat their heads against trees or rocks to try to get these pests to stop bothering them, and

sometimes this may kill the sheep. Other sheep will shake their heads for hours and hours. Some will run until they just drop from running so much. The first time a good shepherd sees this happening to his sheep, he puts oil on the sheep's head and around the nose. This will calm the sheep.

13. Sheep have to have water! A sheep's body is 70 percent water, so water has a lot to do with how healthy and strong a sheep stays. Sheep get their water mainly from three places:

    a. springs and streams

    b. deep wells

    c. dew on the grass (yes, dew on the grass!)

Sheep can go for long periods of time if they can get the dew off the grass early in the morning before the sun evaporates it.

14. Sheep can become "cast down." This means that they get turned over on their back and cannot get up again by themselves. If the shepherd doesn't come to the sheep quickly, the sheep may die! Once the shepherd finds a sheep in this position, he speaks to it  gently and rubs its legs to get its circulation going again. A sheep becomes "cast down" because it's looking for a soft spot, because it has too much wool, or because it's just too fat!

15. In the sheepfold—the place where the sheep sleep—the shepherd lies down in the opening or doorway to guard the sheep. If thieves or predators try to get in and hurt the sheep, they have to cross over the shepherd—because he's the door.*

---

* The information in INSIGHTS ON SHEEP was gathered from Philip Keller, *A Shepherd Looks at Psalm 23* (Grand Rapids, MI: Zondervan Publishing House, 1988). Used by permission.

Week 7:

Getting a Fuller Picture—
Comparing Scripture with
Scripture

Day One

Read John 11 (page 184).

1. Mark any geographical locations and look them up on your map. Watch, too, for time indicators. You will need to go back to John 10:40 and make certain you marked that reference in order to understand where Jesus is in John 11:6.

2. Mark the following key words: *death* (*die, dies, died*), *believe* (*believed, believes*), *life, blind* (remember how you marked this word in John 9 and 10).

Day Two

Read John 11 again.

1. This time mark every reference to the following people: *Lazarus, Jesus, Martha, Mary, the Christ.*

2. List everything you learn about Jesus and Lazarus from this chapter.

Jesus   Lazarus

Day Three

1. Read through John 11 again, and this time list everything you learn about Mary and Martha.

Mary   Martha

2. As I have mentioned before, *when you read the Word of God it is good to compare Scripture with Scripture.* Therefore, in order to gain more insight into Mary and Martha, you will find it helpful to read Luke 10:38-42. As you read, watch for what you can learn about the two sisters. The passage is printed out below, along with

two columns for listing any further things you learn about each of
the women.

> Now as they were traveling along, He entered a village;
> and a woman named Martha welcomed Him into her
> home. She had a sister called Mary, who was seated at
> the Lord's feet, listening to His word. But Martha was
> distracted with all her preparations; and she came up to
> Him and said, "Lord, do You not care that my sister has
> left me to do all the serving alone? Then tell her to help
> me." But the Lord answered and said to her, "Martha,
> Martha, you are worried and bothered about so many
> things; but only one thing is necessary, for Mary has
> chosen the good part, which shall not be taken away
> from her."

Mary	*Martha*

3. Now, thinking of what you saw about Mary and Martha,
answer these questions:

    a. Which woman is more like you? Why?

b. What can you learn from Luke 10:38-42 that you can apply to your own life?

Day Four

1. What do you believe happens to a person when he or she dies?

2. Where did your beliefs come from, or what are they based on?

3. Do you think you can trust them? Why?

4. Let's take a few moments and see what the Word of God says happens when a person dies.

Look up the following references on your Observation Worksheets or in your Bible. (If you don't have a Bible, the references from books other than the Gospel of John are printed out for you.)

As you read these, remember this is the Word of God. Write out (or underline in the references typed out for you) what you learn about people who have believed on the Lord Jesus Christ and therefore have been born again.

    a. John 3:16

    b. John 5:21,24

    c. John 6:37,39,44

    d. John 8:51

e. Philippians 1:21-23:

> To me, to live is Christ and to die is gain. But if I am to live on in the flesh, this will mean fruitful labor for me; and I do not know which to choose. But I am hard-pressed from both directions, having the desire to depart and be with Christ, for that is very much better.

f. John 14:1-3

g. 2 Corinthians 5:8

> We are of good courage, I say, and prefer rather to be absent from the body and to be at home with the Lord.

h. Revelation 21:3-4,6

> I heard a loud voice from the throne, saying, "Behold, the tabernacle of God is among men, and He will dwell among them, and they shall be His people, and God Himself will be among them, and He will wipe away every tear from their eyes; and there shall no longer be any death; there will no longer be any mourning, or crying, or pain; the first things have passed away."...
>
> "I am the Alpha and the Omega, the beginning and the end. I will give to the one who thirsts from the spring of the water of life without cost."

5. Now, how do these words from God compare with your beliefs or the teaching of your religion?

Day Five

1. Today we want to look at what happens to those who do not believe that Jesus is the Christ, the Son of God, and therefore do not have life in His name. Read the following passages in the Bible. Record or underline what you learn about those who do not believe.

    a. John 3:36

    b. John 5:28-29 (Note the contrast here between good and evil deeds. Did you realize that your deeds show who you belong to, who you serve?)

    c. John 8:24

d. Revelation 21:8

For the cowardly and unbelieving and abominable and murderers and immoral persons and sorcerers and idolaters and all liars, their part will be in the lake that burns with fire and brimstone, which is the second death.

e. Revelation 20:11-15

I saw a great white throne and Him who sat upon it, from whose presence earth and heaven fled away, and no place was found for them. And I saw the dead, the great and the small, standing before the throne, and books were opened; and another book was opened, which is the book of life; and the dead were judged from the things which were written in the books, according to their deeds. And the sea gave up the dead which were in it, and death and Hades gave up the dead which were in them; and they were judged, every one of them according to their deeds. Then death and Hades were thrown into the lake of fire. This is the second death, the lake of fire. And if anyone's name was not found written in the book of life, he was thrown into the lake of fire.

2. Now, has this been an eye-opener? You've just looked at what God says about those who do not believe. Summarize what you learned.

3. Make a list of all that you learn from marking the word *believe (believed, believes)* in John 11.

4. Now, beloved one for whom Christ died, have you truly believed? Do your "deeds"—the way you live, you act, you treat people, you obey God's Word—show it?

Isn't it awesome! Jesus loved you and died for you when you were a sinner. He doesn't ask you to change yourself or to clean yourself up; He takes you just the way you are. However, when you come to Him, believing Jesus is God, the Lamb of God who takes away your sins, then He becomes your Shepherd and He gives you eternal life. You will never perish—no one will ever take you out of God's hand. And He will raise you up and you will live with Him forever and ever, for He gives you life—eternal and abundant.

Week 8:

The Importance of Timing—
The Sequence of Events
and What It Leads To

Day One

1. Read John 11:54-57 (page 188). This is a significant passage because it contains important information regarding Jesus and His ministry. Answer the following questions from these verses and record the number of the verse from which you get your answer:

a. WHAT was going to change about Jesus' ministry? Or to put it another way, from WHOM was Jesus withdrawing?

b. WHAT time of year was it? WHAT feast was at hand? Look at your chart on the feasts (page 218) and note when this feast was celebrated.

c. Two groups of people were eager to see Jesus. WHO were they, and WHAT did they want to know?

1)

2)

2. Record the theme of John 11 on the JOHN AT A GLANCE chart (page 217).

3. Read John 12 paragraph by paragraph. (Remember, you can tell where a paragraph begins because the verse number is in darker type.)

As you read through John 12 paragraph by paragraph, watch for and mark two things:

a. As you have done before, mark every reference to time and geographical locations. *This will help you understand the chronological and geographical context of these events. Remember, when we talk about chronological context we are talking about the order or timing of events and how one event follows another.* Don't forget to check the map (page 220) to locate the sites mentioned. Also remember that if God tells us these things in His Word, then He wants us to know them.

b. Notice the various people Jesus comes into contact with in this chapter and their response to Him. In the margin of your Observation Worksheet on John 12, summarize where Jesus is and what He is doing or who He is with.

For example, in the margin at John 12:1 you would write something like this:

> In Bethany
> with Lazarus,
> Mary, Martha

Then next to verses 9-11 you would write,

> Large crowd goes to see Lazarus
> Priests plot Lazarus' death

Doing an exercise like this, looking at a chapter paragraph by paragraph, helps you see everything that is covered in that chapter.

Days Two and Three

1. Read through John 12 again. This time watch for time indicators and locations. Also, you need to mark the key words listed in number 2, which follows. Make sure all of these are on your bookmark. As you mark the words, keep asking the 5 W's and an H.

2. Now make a list of everything you learn about the words you marked. Remember to examine what you learn by asking the 5 W's and an H (WHO, WHAT, WHEN, WHERE, WHY, and HOW). When you ask these questions, get your answers from what the verses say—don't add your own thoughts to them. Then you know you are handling God's Word accurately. (I will give you an example of how to ask the 5 W's and an H on the word *King*).

> a. *King* (Note WHO the king is, of WHOM He is king, WHAT is said about Him, HOW He is going to come, HOW He will be recognized, etc.)

b. *sign (signs)* (Note what sign is being referred to and what the response to the sign[s] was.)

c. *hour*

d. *Son of Man*

e. *believe (believed, believes, believing)*

f. *judge (judges, judgment)*

g. *Light*

    h. *eternal life (life eternal, life)*

    i. *world*

Day Four

1. Read John 13 (see page 192). Watch carefully what events are covered in this chapter, where they take place, what happens, why it happens or is done, what it means, who is pointed out in this chapter, and why. Also observe what Jesus says in this chapter and to whom He says it. Be sure to mark the time indicators and locations as you have before. (In other words, read this chapter and, as you read, keep asking—you guessed it—the 5 W's and an H!)

    Also, watch for and mark any key words you have previously marked. Mark the words *love* and *loved*. (Add these to your bookmark along with the word *loves* since we will look for these in several of the upcoming chapters.)

2. When you finish reading this chapter and doing number 1, write down some of your observations. Be brief and to the point in your answers.

    a. WHAT is this chapter about?

    b. WHO are the major characters in this event, and WHAT do you learn about each of them?

    c. WHY did Jesus wash the disciples' feet? Did He wash the feet of all the disciples? Did He exclude Judas? (What was Judas going to do?) What does this tell you?

   d. WHEN does the event described in John 13 take place? WHY is it at this time?

   e. What lessons or truths does Jesus teach in this chapter and to whom do they apply?

Day Five

1. In John 12:23,27 and 13:1 Jesus refers to "the hour," "this hour," "His hour." From observing the text, what hour do you think Jesus is referring to?

2. Look up the following references in John and note what you learn about each use of the phrase "His (My) hour had (has) not yet come." Note WHEN it is said and WHAT is happening when it is said.

   a. John 2:4

   b. John 7:30

   c. John 8:20

3. Now, in light of what you saw in John 12 and 13 about "the hour," what do you learn about the death of Jesus Christ? Was it an accident or was it planned? And by whom do you think it was planned?

4. According to John 12:23-27, WHY did Jesus come?

5. When we study John 19, we will see in greater detail the way Jesus died. He was crucified. That means He was nailed to a cross and hung there until He died. Look at John 12:32-33. Did Jesus know how He would die? Explain how you know from these verses.

6. Throughout the Gospel of John and the other Gospels (Matthew, Mark, and Luke) Jesus is referred to as "the Son of Man." In John 1:1-3,14 we see that Jesus was God, one with the Father, the Creator of the Earth, the Word of God who became flesh and dwelt among us. Thus, He was also the Son of Man. In other words, God became man. However, because Jesus was born of a virgin, God was His Father; therefore, Jesus was not born with sin as you and I were. Jesus was without sin.

The Gospels of Matthew, Mark, and Luke tell us that Jesus was tempted by the devil just like the first man and woman, Adam and Eve, were tempted. But, unlike Adam and Eve, Jesus did not give in to temptation. He did not sin. As we saw in chapters 5 and 8 of

John, Jesus always and only did what pleased the Father. So He didn't sin. If He had sinned, Jesus would have had to die for His own sin. But because He didn't sin, He could die in our place for our sins—for your sins, for my sins! That is why Jesus became the Son of Man.

In another book of the Bible, Hebrews, we read these verses:

> Since the children share in flesh and blood, He Himself likewise also partook of the same, that through death He might render powerless him who had the power of death, that is, the devil, and might free those who through fear of death were subject to slavery all their lives (Hebrews 2:14-15).

What God is saying is that since you and I are human beings—man—then Jesus became a man, the Son of Man, flesh and blood, for the purpose of dying for us. Our sin gives the devil power over us because the wages or payment for sin is death. When Jesus died for us and paid for our sin, however, He made a way for us to be set free from the devil's power and from death.

Think with me, my friend, about what we have seen thus far in the Gospel of John.

In John 8:34 we learned that whoever commits sin is the slave of sin. In John 8:36, however, we saw that the Son can make us free. We also saw in John 8:44 that the devil is the father of those who do not believe in Jesus, but when we believe Jesus, we believe truth, and God becomes our Father. (Remember, John 1:12 told us that God gives those who receive Jesus the power to become the sons of God.)

To believe in Jesus we have to believe Jesus is God—I AM—and receive Him as our God and Savior, who takes away our sins. The devil's power over us is broken because, as John 12:31 says, the ruler of this world (the devil) is cast out. Our sin has been paid for totally! In full!

When we believe in Jesus and are born again, we are born again into God's family. We then do not continue to live in darkness, but have the light of life, life eternal (John 12:46). Now we are not blind anymore, but have the Light of life. Jesus is the Light of the world (8:12), and we become sons of Light (12:36). We are the fruit of Jesus' death (12:24-25), and we are to serve Him by following Him (12:26). And if we are going to follow Him, we need to serve others—to figuratively "wash their feet" or, to put it another way, to serve them out of love. And how will men know we are disciples (followers) of Jesus Christ? Because we love one another (13:34-35).

7. That's it for this week, Beloved. Good job! Now don't forget to record the themes of John 12 and 13 (page 217).

Oh, Beloved, God does exist. He does care, and so does Jesus. This is why God sent Jesus. It is why Jesus died.

Does He know about you? Abolutely! You are precious to Him—so precious to Him that He crucified His Son for you.

Male or female, child or adult, prisoner or free, of low caste or high caste, educated or uneducated, it matters not to Him. He loves you and wants to be your Father. This is why the Son of Man was lifted up, even as the serpent in the wilderness was lifted up (John 3:14). The serpent represented sin. Jesus was lifted up—on the cross—and God put all your sins, all my sins, all the sins of mankind, on Jesus. And Jesus, who knew no sin, was made sin for us—for you—so that we might have His righteousness.

Salvation, eternal life, freedom from slavery to sin are yours if you will simply believe in the Lord Jesus Christ and receive Him as your God and Savior. Then you will be a child of God forever and ever. Timing is everything: Today is the day of salvation. Take advantage of it. Eternal life can start today.

Think about all that it means...and talk to God about it. You may even want to write out your prayer to Him.

Week 9:

Metaphors, Similes, Allegories, and Parables— So You Get the Picture!

Day One

1. Read John 14 on page 195. Watch for time indicators and locations, and mark the following key words in a distinctive color or way: *love* (*loves*, *loved*), *believe* (*believes*), *Jesus Christ*.

Be sure to mark the pronouns that refer to Jesus Christ. As you mark pronouns, make sure they refer to Jesus and not to someone else.

2. If someone were to ask you what John 14 is about, what would you say at this point?

3. Answer the following questions:

　　a. Jesus Christ is in the Upper Room. WHEN is He saying what He is saying in John 14? If you cannot determine the timing from John 14, then where would you go? That's right—back to John 13.

　　b. To WHOM is He saying these things?

c. WHERE is Judas?

Day Two

1. Read through John 14 again today. This time look for and mark every reference to the *Spirit*. Also mark any pronouns or synonyms that refer to the Spirit. Watch carefully for these.

2. Remember, John's purpose for writing his Gospel was to tell us about some of the signs that Jesus did so that we might believe that Jesus is the Christ, the Son of God, and that believing we might have life in His name.

From this point on, Jesus is not ministering to the public. Instead, He is spending time with His disciples. He wants them to understand the life that He came to give them. So He is going to teach them about this life—what they can expect, how they are to live it, and who will help them.

Therefore, these are very important chapters. If you learn their truths and understand them, then you will know how to live, my friend, and you will have that abundant life Jesus promised in John 10:10—even when you go through trials and tribulation.

Look up John 16:33, which brings Jesus' teaching to His disciples to a close. This verse tells why Jesus spoke "these things" in John 13–16 to His disciples. Write out the reason below, and then keep it in mind as you study these chapters.

3. Make a list of everything you learn about Jesus Christ from John 14. You might want to make this list on a separate piece of paper and then, when you complete it, transfer it to the WHAT JOHN 14–16 TEACHES ABOUT THE FATHER, SON, AND HOLY SPIRIT chart at the end of Week 11 (page 128). This will be a long list, but it is such an important one.

Day Three

1. List everything you learned in John 14 from marking the references to the Holy Spirit. When you finish, transfer this list to the WHAT JOHN 14–16 TEACHES ABOUT THE FATHER, SON, AND HOLY SPIRIT chart at the end of Week 11 (page 128).

2. Now read through John 14 and mark every reference to the *Father*, along with the pronouns and any synonyms that refer to Him. When you finish, make a list on a separate piece of paper of what you learned from John 14 about the Father. Put this information on the WHAT JOHN 14–16 TEACHES ABOUT THE FATHER, SON, AND HOLY SPIRIT chart.

3. Record the theme of John 14 on the JOHN AT A GLANCE chart (page 217).

Day Four

1. Read John 15 (page 197). Look for time indicators and locations and mark every reference to the *Father*, the *Son*, and the *Helper* (or *Spirit of truth*) just as you marked them in John 14.

2. Now read John 15 once more. This time mark the following key words: *abide* (*abides*), *love* (*loved*), *hate* (*hates, hated*), *world*.

Day Five

1. On the WHAT JOHN 14–16 TEACHES ABOUT THE FATHER, SON, AND HOLY SPIRIT chart, list what you learn from John 15 about each person of the Godhead.

2. Today, before we go any further, let's talk for a moment about figures of speech.

A *figure of speech* is a word, a phrase, or an expression used in an imaginative way rather than a literal way. When people write, they often use various types of figures of speech. When you study the Bible, therefore, it is important for you to know when the men who wrote the Bible used figures of speech in order to get their point across.

The most common figures of speech are metaphor, simile, allegory, and parable. They help you get the picture!

- A *metaphor* is an implied comparison. The Gospel of John has a number of them. When Jesus says, "I am the light of the world" or "I am the bread of life," He is using metaphors. These metaphors help explain, in earthly terms, what Jesus is like.

- A *simile* is a comparison of two different things or ideas. A simile will use the words "like," "as," "as...so is," "such as."

- An *allegory* is a description of one thing using the image of another. The example of the vine and the branches in John 15 is an allegory used to teach us about our relationship to Jesus Christ.

- A *parable* is a story that teaches a moral lesson or a truth.

Both parables and allegories are like an extended story that is told to make a point. You see these figures of speech referred to in John 10:6 after Jesus says He is the door to the sheepfold. In John 16:25,29 Jesus talks again about figures of speech.

3. John 15:1-9 is an allegory. List below what you learn from this allegory about:

The Vine   *The Vinedresser*   *The Branches*

4. What is the lesson for us in this allegory in John 15? In answering this, think about the following questions:

    a. To WHOM is Jesus speaking? WHO is with Jesus and WHAT is about to happen to Jesus?

    b. WHO has left the Upper Room in order to go and betray Jesus? Look at John 13:21-30 and write out the answer.

    c. List what you learn about Judas from John 6:66-71 and John 13:18.

    d. Did Judas abide in the vine? Did Judas bear fruit?

    e. For a while, did Judas look like he believed in Jesus Christ? When did it become obvious that he really wasn't a true believer in Jesus Christ?

Do you suppose Jesus told this allegory so the disciples could understand that not everyone who followed Him or said they believed on Him really and truly believed? Taking this allegory in context, it seems that He wanted the disciples to understand that if you belonged to Him, if you were a true believer, a true follower, you would abide in Him and bear fruit. You wouldn't be like Judas.

5. Be sure to record the themes for John 14 and 15 on the JOHN AT A GLANCE chart (page 217).

We have more to learn from John 15, but we will do that next week while we study John 16. Don't forget that John 13–16 all go together, for Jesus is alone with His disciples preparing them for His death, the coming of the Holy Spirit, how they are to live, and what they will face from the world because they belong to Him.

Oh, Beloved, remember…these are God's words, written and preserved for you so you can know how to have eternal life and how to live in this world until Jesus Christ returns to Earth to rule as King of kings and Lord of lords. Abide in Him—the words that He speaks are spirit and life (John 6:63)!

Week 10:
Topical Studies—Getting the Whole Counsel of God on a Subject

Day One

1. Read John 14–15 again (page 195). As you read, you will see Jesus is speaking to the 11 disciples after He washed their feet at supper. Mark every reference to the 11 disciples. Watch for and mark the pronouns that refer to them, especially the word *you*.

Day Two

1. Make a list of everything you learn from marking the references to the 11 disciples in John 14–15. Transfer this list to the WHAT JOHN 14–16 TEACHES ABOUT THOSE WHO COME TO THE FATHER THROUGH THE SON chart at the end of Week 11 (page 129).

2. Do you think what you have listed about the 11 disciples should be true of you also if you belong to the Lord Jesus Christ? Why?

Day Three

1. Read John 16 (page 199). Look for time indicators and locations and mark every reference to *God* (the Father), *Jesus Christ*, and the *Holy Spirit*. Watch for the synonyms and pronouns that refer to each of these and make sure you mark them. You don't want to miss one single precious truth. Also mark the key words *believe, loves (loved)*.

2. Now list everything you learn from marking the references to Jesus Christ in John 16 on the WHAT JOHN 14–16 TEACHES ABOUT THE FATHER, SON, AND HOLY SPIRIT (page 128).

Day Four

1. Read through John 16 again. This time mark every reference to the 11 disciples whom Jesus chose.

2. List everything you learn from John 16 about the Father and the Holy Spirit. Record your list on the chart on page 128. As you compile your list, watch for the three things the Holy Spirit will do when He comes.

Examine all this with the 5 W's and an H. Note WHERE the Spirit comes to, WHAT He does, and WHY. You might want to mark these three things in the text simply by putting a number above each one. This is a good way to mark lists right in your Bible. It helps you observe the text closely and to remember what God says.

Day Five

1. Read through John 16 again. This is such an important chapter for you personally, Beloved, as are John 14 and 15. List what you learn from marking the references to the 11 disciples on the WHAT JOHN 14–16 TEACHES ABOUT THOSE WHO COME TO THE FATHER THROUGH THE SON chart (page 129).

2. A helpful exercise to do in your Bible study is to compile truth on various topics. This begins with making topical lists by

looking up everything the Bible teaches on a particular subject. A topical list is a list of all the facts or information the Bible gives on a certain subject, event, or person. Topical lists must be done very carefully, however.

As I said earlier, it is always vital to understand the context in which something is taught, something is said, or something occurs. (Remember, *context* is the setting in which something is taught, said, or occurs.) When it comes to interpreting the Scripture—discerning what it means—context must always rule. Scripture will never contradict Scripture. So our task as students of the Bible is to discover what the Word of God teaches on any given subject through thorough and careful observation of the whole teaching of God's Word.

You begin doing this by studying the Bible book by book. Reading the Bible through over and over enables you to *keep the "whole teaching"—the whole counsel—of God's Word before you.* This will help you understand context and enable you to properly interpret Scripture.*

---

* The principles of study that you have learned from doing this study on John can be applied to any book of the Bible. To help you do this I have written a number of other studies, each requiring a different commitment of time. However, the very best place to begin is by purchasing *The New Inductive Study Bible*. This Bible has instructions at the beginning of each book of the Bible that will tell you THINGS TO DO that will help you understand that particular book. There are also numerous other wonderful study helps. If you have *The New Inductive Study Bible*, you will be able to study God's Word on your own for the rest of your life.

There's also another book, *Discovering the Bible for Yourself*, that is a great tool for analyzing the Bible book by book. This book and *How to Study Your Bible* are valuable tools used by multitudes in many languages.

We also offer a series called THE NEW INDUCTIVE STUDY SERIES which helps you do a survey of various books of the Bible. Plus, we have PRECEPT UPON PRECEPT BIBLE STUDY COURSES available in more than 65 languages. If you want more information, contact Precept Ministries, P.O. Box 182218, Chattanooga, TN 37422, or visit us online at precept.org. Also see the descriptions of these items on the final pages of this book.

Look up the following passages and see what they teach about the Holy Spirit. Then add these insights to the chart on page 128 at the end of Week 11.

    a. John 1:32-33

    b. John 3:5-6,8

    c. John 3:34

    d. John 4:23-24

    e. John 6:63

    f. John 7:38-39

    g. John 20:22

3. According to what you have learned from John, if you believe on the Lord Jesus Christ, where is the Holy Spirit in relationship to you? Review all you have learned about the Holy Spirit (check your chart on page 128). And then thank God the Spirit for all that He will do for you and tell Him you want to remember this and live in the light of these truths.

Week 11:
Set Apart by Truth, Kept by Prayer

Day One

Read John 17 (page 202). When you finish, ask the 5 W's and an H about this chapter and record your insights below. Make sure you cover WHO is speaking, to WHOM, and WHAT He is speaking about.

I am not going to help you with any more than this because it is good for you to think on your own. Then in the future you will be able to apply these same principles to other books of the Bible when you study them.

Day Two

Read through John 17 again and look for and mark time indicators and locations. Also mark the following key words: *world*, *word(s)*, *eternal life*, *love*, and *Jesus Christ* (be sure to mark every reference, including pronouns).

Day Three

1. Read John 17 again, marking the following key words and phrases:

a. *all whom You have given Him* or *whom You have given Me*

b. every reference to the 11 disciples

c. the reference to *Judas* (In verse 12 he is called the *son of perdition*.)

d. *one*

e. *glory (glorified, glorify)*

f. *love*

2. Do you think this "prayer" of Jesus to the Father was just for the 11 disciples, or do its truths apply to you also? Now that you have marked the text of John 17, read through it again and think about this question. Write down your answer.

Day Four

1. Read through John 17 again. Reading the chapter aloud will help you remember it. As a matter of fact, when you read Scripture aloud over and over again, you will find yourself automatically remembering it.

What a blessing it is to memorize Scripture! Because when you do, you always have it with you. And having truth in your mind and heart allows you to meditate on it—to think it over and to think about how it applies to your life and what you should or should not believe.

If you want to memorize something, simply read it aloud three times at three different times each day for a week. (That's a total of nine times a day for seven days—63 times!) You'll have it memorized by the end of the week.

2. Now make a list of everything you learn from marking the references to Jesus in this chapter. Record your insights, as you have done before, on the chart WHAT JOHN 14–16 TEACHES ABOUT THE FATHER, SON, AND HOLY SPIRIT at the end of this lesson (page 128).

Day Five

1. Go through John 17 verse by verse and make a list of everything Jesus says about and prays for the 11 disciples. Then make a list of what He prays for or says about those who believe on Him through their (the disciples') word (message).

The Eleven	*Those Who Believe* *Through Their Word*

The Eleven

Those Who Believe
Through Their Word

2. Now, beloved student, think of the setting of John 17. Jesus is praying to His Father on your behalf just before He goes to the Garden of Gethsemane, where He will be arrested and taken to the house of Caiaphas, the high priest—who, along with his father-in-law, Annas, wants to get rid of Jesus.

    a. From all that you have seen since you started studying John 13, who is uppermost on Jesus' heart?

    b. What does this tell you about Jesus?

    c. What does this tell you about what Jesus thinks or feels about you?

3. Use what you learn from John 17:14-17 to answer the following:

    a. What is the importance of studying the Bible?

b. What does it tell you about the Bible?

c. When you finish this study are you going to study the Bible? Why?

4. Record the theme of John 17.

We only have two more weeks of study, and then you will have finished the work you began. I am so very proud of you. What a joy it is to write this for you. How we have prayed for you. How I wish I could tell you face-to-face how precious you are to God and how He longs to bless you if you will only believe Him and live according to His Word by the power of His indwelling Holy Spirit. Remember—stay in the Word. It's truth that sets you apart from the world, the culture.

What John 14–16 Teaches About
the Father, Son, and Holy Spirit

The Father   *The Son*   *The Holy Spirit*

**What John 14–16 Teaches About Those
Who Come to the Father Through the Son**

Week 12:

Life? The Word?
It's All About Jesus

Day One

1. Read through John 18 (page 204) and record in the margin of your Observation Worksheet what happens in each paragraph and where it happens.

Remember, each paragraph begins with a verse number that is printed in darker print. However, in verse 38 you will see that the number 38 is not bold, but the "A" of the word "And" is bold. When you read it you will understand why the paragraph begins there.

Remember, a paragraph is a group of sentences that are grouped together because they have something in common. They may focus on a certain thought or event.

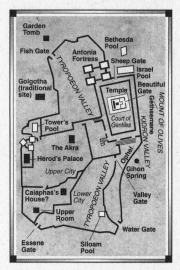

2. As you read through John 18, mark all references to time and geographical locations in the same way you marked them before. In this chapter all the events take place in Jerusalem, but they happen in different places in the city. Mark these different places in Jerusalem.

Consult the map on the previous page that shows Jerusalem at the time of Jesus so you can see the geographical relationship of these places.

3. Mark the following words: *truth, king, kingdom.* (You marked *king* in chapter12, so mark it here the same way you did there. Mark *kingdom* differently.)

Day Two

Read John 19 (page 207) and follow the same instructions you were given yesterday for chapter 18.

1. Mark all references to time.

2. Mark the following words: *sin, truth,* and *king.*

Day Three

Today I want you to read through John 18 again paragraph by paragraph, but this time I want you to focus on those individuals who interact with Jesus.

Watch what each does and how Jesus responds to them. If any reason is given for why Jesus responds as He does, note this. Record below what you learn.

    a. Jesus and Judas

b. Jesus and Peter

c. Jesus and the high priest and his officers

d. Jesus and Pilate

Day Four

Read through John 19 today and, as you did yesterday, record what you learn about the people who interact with Jesus and how He responds to them.

    a. Jesus and Pilate (Add this to the list you began under Day Three.)

    b. Jesus and the Jews

    c. Jesus and the chief priests

    d. Jesus and the soldiers

e. Jesus and His mother

f. Jesus and Joseph of Arimathea

g. Jesus and Nicodemus (Remember Nicodemus from John 3? What does this imply about Nicodemus?)

Day Five

1. Look at the key words you marked this week—*sin, truth, king,* and *kingdom*—and make a list of what you learned from marking each of these words in John 18–19.

Sin	*Truth*	*King*	*Kingdom*

2. Record the themes of John 18 and 19 on the JOHN AT A GLANCE chart (page 217).

3. Read through John 18–19 again. Think about all that happened and picture the events in your mind. As you do, remember Jesus is God. He could have stopped them from beating Him and crucifying Him, but He didn't. Why? Because He cares about you. Someone must pay for sin. Jesus was born to die for your sins, my sins—the sins of all mankind.

Jesus is the grain of wheat who would fall into the ground and die so that He would not abide alone but bring forth the fruit of eternal life for others. (Note the metaphor.)

He is the Good Shepherd who laid down His life for His sheep (again, note the metaphor).

He is the Lamb of God who takes away the sins of the world—the Passover Lamb, slain on the very day they celebrated the Passover and killed the Passover lambs (see John 18:39).

He is the Light of the World hanging on the cross—the light the religious leaders wanted to extinguish.

He is the One who called those who were thirsty to come and drink of Him.

He is the King who rode into Jerusalem on a donkey as the fulfillment of Zechariah's prophecy: "Rejoice greatly, O daughter of Zion!...Behold, your king is coming to you...humble, and mounted on a donkey, even on a colt..." (Zechariah 9:9).

He is the Son of Man dying in mankind's place—in your place. The One who came to explain the Father to us—the Father who "so loved the world, that He gave His only begotten Son, that whoever believes in Him shall not perish, but have eternal life" (John 3:16). *Life? It's all about Jesus!*

Fall at His feet and say, "My Lord and my God! You are there! You do care! You know about me!" Worship Him!

Week 13:

Wrapping It Up—
Putting On
the Belt of Truth

Day One

Read from John 19:38 through John 20:31. Move through it paragraph by paragraph. Note where the action takes place, who is involved, when it occurs, etc.

Day Two

1. Read through John 20 (page 210), looking for time indicators and locations.

2. Mark the following key words: *peace, believe (believed, believing), sins, risen (risen from the dead), ascend (ascended)*.

Note that there is a difference between rising from the dead and ascending. What is the difference?

3. Now, below, list all you learn from marking each of the key words.

Day Three

1. Read John 2:13-22.

    a. How does what happened in this passage relate to the main event of John 20?

    b. WHAT was the final sign, the sign of signs, God gave to prove that Jesus is the Christ, the Son of God—the giver of eternal life?

    c. Did anyone witness this final sign? WHO? WHEN?

2. If you have time and have access to a Bible, it would be good for you to read the other Gospel accounts of the death, burial, and resurrection of our Lord Jesus Christ. You will find these in Matthew 27–28; Mark 14–16; Luke 22–24.

3. Read 1 Corinthians 15:1-8 printed out for you here and listen to what the apostle Paul would later write about the gospel (the good news) about Jesus Christ. As you read, put a symbol like this ◁ʘ over the word *gospel*, and its pronouns. Underline *of first importance*. Then circle each occurrence of *that*.

> Now I make known to you, brethren, the gospel which
> I preached to you, which also you received, in which
> also you stand, by which also you are saved, if you hold
> fast the word which I preached to you, unless you
> believed in vain.
>
> For I delivered to you as of first importance what I also
> received, that Christ died for our sins according to the
> Scriptures, and that He was buried, and that He was
> raised on the third day according to the Scriptures, and
> that He appeared to Cephas,* then to the twelve. After
> that He appeared to more than five hundred brethren at
> one time, most of whom remain until now, but some
> have fallen asleep; then He appeared to James, then to
> all the apostles; and last of all, as to one untimely born,
> He appeared to me also (1 Corinthians 15:1-8).

Paul reminds us that Jesus died according to the Scriptures and was raised the third day according to the Scriptures. "According to the Scriptures" means that Jesus' death and resurrection were both prophesied in the Old Testament, hundreds of years before these events ever happened. Then, "when the fullness of the time came, God sent forth His Son, born of a woman...so that He might redeem" you and me, Beloved (Galatians 4:4-5). Oh, what love God has bestowed upon us!

Day Four

1. Read John 21 (page 213). Move through it paragraph by paragraph, noting what happens in each paragraph, who is involved, when and where it takes place. Make these notes in the margin of your Observation Worksheet.

---

* *Cephas* is another name for Peter.

2. Read John 21 again. Look for time indicators and locations, and mark the following key words: *love (loved)*, *sheep (lambs)*, *testify (testifies)*, *testimony*, *manifested* (watch for what or who was manifested, how and when).

3. List what you learn from marking these key words.

4. What do you learn from this chapter about

    a. Peter

    b. John (the one who wrote this Gospel)

5. Go back to John 18 and read verses 15-27. Answer the following questions by comparing these verses with John 21.

    a. Where was Peter standing when he denied Jesus Christ?

    b. Where was Peter standing when Jesus talked with him in John 21:9-19?

    c. Although Peter denied Jesus three times in John 18, what did Peter get to tell Jesus three times in John 21?

    d. What did Peter tell Jesus he would do for Him in John 13:37?

    e. When Jesus was arrested, however, what did Peter do?

f.   According to John 21, what would Peter get to do?

g.   Would he deny Jesus again in the face of arrest and death?

Now, Beloved, even when in our weakness we might deny Jesus temporarily, does Jesus still care? Does He still love us, still want us? How do you know from John 21?

6. Record the themes of John 20 and 21.

Day Five

1. Turn to your JOHN AT A GLANCE chart in the appendix and look at it carefully. This chart helps you wrap up the Gospel of John in a neat package of truth. It would be good review for you to go through John chapter by chapter and see what you recorded as the theme of each chapter. If you want to change any, do so at this point. If you missed recording a theme for any chapter, do that now.

2. Fill in any other information that you have not yet recorded. You know who wrote the book and why, so be sure to fill in Author and Purpose. I'll give you the date the book was written: about A.D. 85. You can also list the key words, since you have marked those in each chapter! Add any you discovered on your own to the list.

3. Consider the author's purpose for writing once again. What statement best describes the book as a whole? That should be your theme for the Gospel of John, so record it in the appropriate spot on the chart.

4. Now, it would be a wonderful exercise for you to go through the first 11 chapters of John and see what signs were performed by Jesus and recorded by John. Note these under Segment Divisions in the boxes labeled "Signs and Miracles." Put each miracle under the number of the chapter in which it occurred.

5. Jesus is portrayed in a number of different ways throughout the Gospel of John. For instance, He is the Light of the world, the Bread of life, the Shepherd of the sheep, the Vine, the Resurrection and the Life. Think about these portrayals and then record these under the Segment Divisions in the boxes labeled "Portrayals of Jesus." Put each portrayal under the number of the chapter in which it occurred.

Congratulations, Beloved! You've finished your study of the Gospel of John. Just think, this Gospel was written for you, "so that you may believe that Jesus is the Christ, the Son of God; and that believing you may have life in His name."

Does God exist? Is He there? Oh, yes! Jesus has shown Him to us and has explained Him. God is there and always will be.

Does He care? Oh, yes! He gave you the greatest of gifts—His only begotten Son.

Does He know about you? Oh, yes! Beloved, He knows. Enough to come to you right where you are—to put this book into your hands so that you might know Him, love Him, and follow Him no matter what anyone else says or does.

Will you, Beloved?

And will you take what you've learned and share it with another person who needs to discover the answers to these questions for themselves? Think of the ministry you can have with this book, which is being used all over the world to bring people to Christ, to teach them how to "discover truth for yourself," and to establish churches.

Appendixes

Observation Worksheets:

The Gospel
of John

Chapter 1

1 In the beginning was the Word, and the Word was with God, and the Word was God.

2 He was in the beginning with God.

3 All things came into being through Him, and apart from Him nothing came into being that has come into being.

4 In Him was life, and the life was the Light of men.

5 The Light shines in the darkness, and the darkness did not comprehend it.

6 There came a man sent from God, whose name was John.

7 He came as a witness, to testify about the Light, so that all might believe through him.

8 He was not the Light, but *he came* to testify about the Light.

9 There was the true Light which, coming into the world, enlightens every man.

10 He was in the world, and the world was made through Him, and the world did not know Him.

11 He came to His own, and those who were His own did not receive Him.

12 But as many as received Him, to them He gave the right to become children of God, *even* to those who believe in His name,

13 who were born, not of blood nor of the will of the flesh nor of the will of man, but of God.

14 And the Word became flesh, and dwelt among us, and we saw His glory, glory as of the only begotten from the Father, full of grace and truth.

15 John testified about Him and cried out, saying, "This was He of whom I said, 'He who comes after me has a higher rank than I, for He existed before me.'"

16 For of His fullness we have all received, and grace upon grace.

17 For the Law was given through Moses; grace and truth were realized through Jesus Christ.

18 No one has seen God at any time; the only begotten God who is in the bosom of the Father, He has explained *Him*.

19 This is the testimony of John, when the Jews sent to him priests and Levites from Jerusalem to ask him, "Who are you?"

20 And he confessed and did not deny, but confessed, "I am not the Christ."

21 They asked him, "What then? Are you Elijah?" And he said, "I am not." "Are you the Prophet?" And he answered, "No."

22 Then they said to him, "Who are you, so that we may give an answer to those who sent us? What do you say about yourself?"

23 He said, "I am A VOICE OF ONE CRYING IN THE WILDERNESS, 'MAKE STRAIGHT THE WAY OF THE LORD,' as Isaiah the prophet said."

24 Now they had been sent from the Pharisees.

25 They asked him, and said to him, "Why then are you baptizing, if you are not the Christ, nor Elijah, nor the Prophet?"

26 John answered them saying, "I baptize in water, *but* among you stands One whom you do not know.

27 "*It is* He who comes after me, the thong of whose sandal I am not worthy to untie."

28 These things took place in Bethany beyond the Jordan, where John was baptizing.

29 The next day he saw Jesus coming to him and said, "Behold, the Lamb of God who takes away the sin of the world!

30 "This is He on behalf of whom I said, 'After me comes a Man who has a higher rank than I, for He existed before me.'

31 "I did not recognize Him, but so that He might be manifested to Israel, I came baptizing in water."

32 John testified saying, "I have seen the Spirit descending as a dove out of heaven, and He remained upon Him.

33 "I did not recognize Him, but He who sent me to baptize in water said to me, 'He upon whom you see the Spirit descending and remaining upon Him, this is the One who baptizes in the Holy Spirit.'

34 "I myself have seen, and have testified that this is the Son of God."

35 Again the next day John was standing with two of his disciples,

36 and he looked at Jesus as He walked, and said, "Behold, the Lamb of God!"

37 The two disciples heard him speak, and they followed Jesus.

38 And Jesus turned and saw them following, and said to them, "What do you seek?" They said to Him, "Rabbi (which translated means Teacher), where are You staying?"

39 He said to them, "Come, and you will see." So they came and saw where He was staying; and they stayed with Him that day, for it was about the tenth hour.

40 One of the two who heard John *speak* and followed Him, was Andrew, Simon Peter's brother.

41 He found first his own brother Simon and said to him, "We have found the Messiah" (which translated means Christ).

42 He brought him to Jesus. Jesus looked at him and said, "You are Simon the son of John; you shall be called Cephas" (which is translated Peter).

43 The next day He purposed to go into Galilee, and He found Philip. And Jesus said to him, "Follow Me."

44 Now Philip was from Bethsaida, of the city of Andrew and Peter.

45 Philip found Nathanael and said to him, "We have found Him of whom Moses in the Law and *also* the Prophets wrote—Jesus of Nazareth, the son of Joseph."

46 Nathanael said to him, "Can any good thing come out of Nazareth?" Philip said to him, "Come and see."

47 Jesus saw Nathanael coming to Him, and said of him, "Behold, an Israelite indeed, in whom there is no deceit!"

48 Nathanael said to Him, "How do You know me?" Jesus answered and said to him, "Before Philip called you, when you were under the fig tree, I saw you."

49 Nathanael answered Him, "Rabbi, You are the Son of God; You are the King of Israel."

50 Jesus answered and said to him, "Because I said to you that I saw you under the fig tree, do you believe? You will see greater things than these."

51 And He said to him, "Truly, truly, I say to you, you will see the heavens opened and the angels of God ascending and descending on the Son of Man."

Chapter 2

1 On the third day there was a wedding in Cana of Galilee, and the mother of Jesus was there;

2 and both Jesus and His disciples were invited to the wedding.

3 When the wine ran out, the mother of Jesus said to Him, "They have no wine."

4 And Jesus said to her, "Woman, what does that have to do with us? My hour has not yet come."

5 His mother said to the servants, "Whatever He says to you, do it."

6 Now there were six stone waterpots set there for the Jewish custom of purification, containing twenty or thirty gallons each.

7 Jesus said to them, "Fill the waterpots with water." So they filled them up to the brim.

8 And He said to them, "Draw *some* out now and take it to the headwaiter." So they took it *to him*.

9 When the headwaiter tasted the water which had become wine, and did not know where it came from (but the servants who had drawn the water knew), the headwaiter called the bridegroom,

10 and said to him, "Every man serves the good wine first, and when *the people* have drunk freely, *then he serves* the poorer *wine; but* you have kept the good wine until now."

11 This beginning of *His* signs Jesus did in Cana of Galilee, and manifested His glory, and His disciples believed in Him.

12 After this He went down to Capernaum, He and His mother and *His* brothers and His disciples; and they stayed there a few days.

13 The Passover of the Jews was near, and Jesus went up to Jerusalem.

14 And He found in the temple those who were selling oxen and sheep and doves, and the money changers seated *at their tables*.

15 And He made a scourge of cords, and drove *them* all out of the temple, with the sheep and the oxen; and He poured out the coins of the money changers and overturned their tables;

16 and to those who were selling the doves He said, "Take these things away; stop making My Father's house a place of business."

17 His disciples remembered that it was written, "ZEAL FOR YOUR HOUSE WILL CONSUME ME."

18 The Jews then said to Him, "What sign do You show us as your authority for doing these things?"

19 Jesus answered them, "Destroy this temple, and in three days I will raise it up."

20 The Jews then said, "It took forty-six years to build this temple, and will You raise it up in three days?"

21 But He was speaking of the temple of His body.

22 So when He was raised from the dead, His disciples remembered that He said this; and they believed the Scripture and the word which Jesus had spoken.

23 Now when He was in Jerusalem at the Passover, during the feast, many believed in His name, observing His signs which He was doing.

24 But Jesus, on His part, was not entrusting Himself to them, for He knew all men,

25 and because He did not need anyone to testify concerning man, for He Himself knew what was in man.

Chapter 3

1 Now there was a man of the Pharisees, named Nicodemus, a ruler of the Jews;

2 this man came to Jesus by night and said to Him, "Rabbi, we know that You have come from God as a teacher; for no one can do these signs that You do unless God is with him."

3 Jesus answered and said to him, "Truly, truly, I say to you, unless one is born again he cannot see the kingdom of God."

4 Nicodemus said to Him, "How can a man be born when he is old? He cannot enter a second time into his mother's womb and be born, can he?"

5 Jesus answered, "Truly, truly, I say to you, unless one is born of water and the Spirit he cannot enter into the kingdom of God.

6 "That which is born of the flesh is flesh, and that which is born of the Spirit is spirit.

7 "Do not be amazed that I said to you, 'You must be born again.'

8 "The wind blows where it wishes and you hear the sound of it, but do not know where it comes from and where it is going; so is everyone who is born of the Spirit."

9 Nicodemus said to Him, "How can these things be?"

10 Jesus answered and said to him, "Are you the teacher of Israel and do not understand these things?

11 "Truly, truly, I say to you, we speak of what we know and testify of what we have seen, and you do not accept our testimony.

12 "If I told you earthly things and you do not believe, how will you believe if I tell you heavenly things?

13 "No one has ascended into heaven, but He who descended from heaven: the Son of Man.

14 "As Moses lifted up the serpent in the wilderness, even so must the Son of Man be lifted up;

15 so that whoever believes will in Him have eternal life.

16 "For God so loved the world, that He gave His only begotten Son, that whoever believes in Him shall not perish, but have eternal life.

17 "For God did not send the Son into the world to judge the world, but that the world might be saved through Him.

18 "He who believes in Him is not judged; he who does not believe has been judged already, because he has not believed in the name of the only begotten Son of God.

19 "This is the judgment, that the Light has come into the world, and men loved the darkness rather than the Light, for their deeds were evil.

20 "For everyone who does evil hates the Light, and does not come to the Light for fear that his deeds will be exposed.

21 "But he who practices the truth comes to the Light, so that his deeds may be manifested as having been wrought in God."

22 After these things Jesus and His disciples came into the land of Judea, and there He was spending time with them and baptizing.

23 John also was baptizing in Aenon near Salim, because there was much water there; and *people* were coming and were being baptized—

24 for John had not yet been thrown into prison.

25 Therefore there arose a discussion on the part of John's disciples with a Jew about purification.

26 And they came to John and said to him, "Rabbi, He who was with you beyond the Jordan, to whom you have testified, behold, He is baptizing and all are coming to Him."

27 John answered and said, "A man can receive nothing unless it has been given him from heaven.

28 "You yourselves are my witnesses that I said, 'I am not the Christ,' but, 'I have been sent ahead of Him.'

29 "He who has the bride is the bridegroom; but the friend of the bridegroom, who stands and hears him, rejoices greatly because of the bridegroom's voice. So this joy of mine has been made full.

30 "He must increase, but I must decrease.

31 "He who comes from above is above all, he who is of the earth is from the earth and speaks of the earth. He who comes from heaven is above all.

32 "What He has seen and heard, of that He testifies; and no one receives His testimony.

33 "He who has received His testimony has set his seal to *this*, that God is true.

34 "For He whom God has sent speaks the words of God; for He gives the Spirit without measure.

35 "The Father loves the Son and has given all things into His hand.

36 "He who believes in the Son has eternal life; but he who does not obey the Son will not see life, but the wrath of God abides on him."

Chapter 4

1 Therefore when the Lord knew that the Pharisees had heard that Jesus was making and baptizing more disciples than John

2 (although Jesus Himself was not baptizing, but His disciples were),

3 He left Judea and went away again into Galilee.

4 And He had to pass through Samaria.

5 So He came to a city of Samaria called Sychar, near the parcel of ground that Jacob gave to his son Joseph;

6 and Jacob's well was there. So Jesus, being wearied from His journey, was sitting thus by the well. It was about the sixth hour.

7 There came a woman of Samaria to draw water. Jesus said to her, "Give Me a drink."

8 For His disciples had gone away into the city to buy food.

9 Therefore the Samaritan woman said to Him, "How is it that You, being a Jew, ask me for a drink since I am a Samaritan woman?" (For Jews have no dealings with Samaritans.)

10 Jesus answered and said to her, "If you knew the gift of God, and who it is who says to you, 'Give Me a drink,' you would have asked Him, and He would have given you living water."

11 She said to Him, "Sir, You have nothing to draw with and the well is deep; where then do You get that living water?

12 "You are not greater than our father Jacob, are You, who gave us the well, and drank of it himself and his sons and his cattle?"

13 Jesus answered and said to her, "Everyone who drinks of this water will thirst again;

14 but whoever drinks of the water that I will give him shall never thirst; but the water that I will give him will become in him a well of water springing up to eternal life."

15 The woman said to Him, "Sir, give me this water, so I will not be thirsty nor come all the way here to draw."

16 He said to her, "Go, call your husband and come here."

17 The woman answered and said, "I have no husband." Jesus said to her, "You have correctly said, 'I have no husband';

18 for you have had five husbands, and the one whom you now have is not your husband; this you have said truly."

19 The woman said to Him, "Sir, I perceive that You are a prophet.

20 "Our fathers worshiped in this mountain, and you *people* say that in Jerusalem is the place where men ought to worship."

21 Jesus said to her, "Woman, believe Me, an hour is coming when neither in this mountain nor in Jerusalem will you worship the Father.

22 "You worship what you do not know; we worship what we know, for salvation is from the Jews.

23 "But an hour is coming, and now is, when the true worshipers will worship the Father in spirit and truth; for such people the Father seeks to be His worshipers.

24 "God is spirit, and those who worship Him must worship in spirit and truth."

25 The woman said to Him, "I know that Messiah is coming (He who is called Christ); when that One comes, He will declare all things to us."

26 Jesus said to her, "I who speak to you am *He*."

27 At this point His disciples came, and they were amazed that He had been speaking with a woman, yet no one said, "What do You seek?" or, "Why do You speak with her?"

28 So the woman left her waterpot, and went into the city and said to the men,

29 "Come, see a man who told me all the things that I *have* done; this is not the Christ, is it?"

30 They went out of the city, and were coming to Him.

31 Meanwhile the disciples were urging Him, saying, "Rabbi, eat."

32 But He said to them, "I have food to eat that you do not know about."

33 So the disciples were saying to one another, "No one brought Him *anything* to eat, did he?"

34 Jesus said to them, "My food is to do the will of Him who sent Me and to accomplish His work.

35 "Do you not say, 'There are yet four months, and *then* comes the harvest'? Behold, I say to you, lift up your eyes and look on the fields, that they are white for harvest.

36 "Already he who reaps is receiving wages and is gathering fruit for life eternal; so that he who sows and he who reaps may rejoice together.

37 "For in this *case* the saying is true, 'One sows and another reaps.'

38 "I sent you to reap that for which you have not labored; others have labored and you have entered into their labor."

39 From that city many of the Samaritans believed in Him because of the word of the woman who testified, "He told me all the things that I *have* done."

40 So when the Samaritans came to Jesus, they were asking Him to stay with them; and He stayed there two days.

41 Many more believed because of His word;

42 and they were saying to the woman, "It is no longer because of what you said that we believe, for we have heard for ourselves and know that this One is indeed the Savior of the world."

43 After the two days He went forth from there into Galilee.

44 For Jesus Himself testified that a prophet has no honor in his own country.

45 So when He came to Galilee, the Galileans received Him, having seen all the things that He did in Jerusalem at the feast; for they themselves also went to the feast.

46 Therefore He came again to Cana of Galilee where He had made the water wine. And there was a royal official whose son was sick at Capernaum.

47 When he heard that Jesus had come out of Judea into Galilee, he went to Him and was imploring *Him* to come down and heal his son; for he was at the point of death.

48 So Jesus said to him, "Unless you *people* see signs and wonders, you *simply* will not believe."

49 The royal official said to Him, "Sir, come down before my child dies."

50 Jesus said to him, "Go; your son lives." The man believed the word that Jesus spoke to him and started off.

51 As he was now going down, *his* slaves met him, saying that his son was living.

52 So he inquired of them the hour when he began to get better. Then they said to him, "Yesterday at the seventh hour the fever left him."

53 So the father knew that *it was* at that hour in which Jesus said to him, "Your son lives"; and he himself believed and his whole household.

54 This is again a second sign that Jesus performed when He had come out of Judea into Galilee.

Chapter 5

1 After these things there was a feast of the Jews, and Jesus went up to Jerusalem.

2 Now there is in Jerusalem by the sheep *gate* a pool, which is called in Hebrew Bethesda, having five porticoes.

3 In these lay a multitude of those who were sick, blind, lame, and withered, [waiting for the moving of the waters;

4 for an angel of the Lord went down at certain seasons into the pool and stirred up the water; whoever then first, after the stirring up of the water, stepped in was made well from whatever disease with which he was afflicted.]

5 A man was there who had been ill for thirty-eight years.

6 When Jesus saw him lying *there*, and knew that he had already been a long time *in that condition*, He said to him, "Do you wish to get well?"

7 The sick man answered Him, "Sir, I have no man to put me into the pool when the water is stirred up, but while I am coming, another steps down before me."

8 Jesus said to him, "Get up, pick up your pallet and walk."

9 Immediately the man became well, and picked up his pallet and *began* to walk.

Now it was the Sabbath on that day.

10 So the Jews were saying to the man who was cured, "It is the Sabbath, and it is not permissible for you to carry your pallet."

11 But he answered them, "He who made me well was the one who said to me, 'Pick up your pallet and walk.'"

12 They asked him, "Who is the man who said to you, 'Pick up *your pallet* and walk'?"

13 But the man who was healed did not know who it was, for Jesus had slipped away while there was a crowd in *that* place.

14 Afterward Jesus found him in the temple and said to him, "Behold, you have become well; do not sin anymore, so that nothing worse happens to you."

15 The man went away, and told the Jews that it was Jesus who had made him well.

16 For this reason the Jews were persecuting Jesus, because He was doing these things on the Sabbath.

17 But He answered them, "My Father is working until now, and I Myself am working."

18 For this reason therefore the Jews were seeking all the more to kill Him, because He not only was breaking the Sabbath, but also was calling God His own Father, making Himself equal with God.

19 Therefore Jesus answered and was saying to them, "Truly, truly, I say to you, the Son can do nothing of Himself, unless *it is*

something He sees the Father doing; for whatever the Father does, these things the Son also does in like manner.

20 "For the Father loves the Son, and shows Him all things that He Himself is doing; and *the Father* will show Him greater works than these, so that you will marvel.

21 "For just as the Father raises the dead and gives them life, even so the Son also gives life to whom He wishes.

22 "For not even the Father judges anyone, but He has given all judgment to the Son,

23 so that all will honor the Son even as they honor the Father. He who does not honor the Son does not honor the Father who sent Him.

24 "Truly, truly, I say to you, he who hears My word, and believes Him who sent Me, has eternal life, and does not come into judgment, but has passed out of death into life.

25 "Truly, truly, I say to you, an hour is coming and now is, when the dead will hear the voice of the Son of God, and those who hear will live.

26 "For just as the Father has life in Himself, even so He gave to the Son also to have life in Himself;

27 and He gave Him authority to execute judgment, because He is *the* Son of Man.

28 "Do not marvel at this; for an hour is coming, in which all who are in the tombs will hear His voice,

29 and will come forth; those who did the good *deeds* to a resurrection of life, those who committed the evil *deeds* to a resurrection of judgment.

30 "I can do nothing on My own initiative. As I hear, I judge; and My judgment is just, because I do not seek My own will, but the will of Him who sent Me.

31 "If I *alone* testify about Myself, My testimony is not true.

32 "There is another who testifies of Me, and I know that the testimony which He gives about Me is true.

33 "You have sent to John, and he has testified to the truth.

34 "But the testimony which I receive is not from man, but I say these things so that you may be saved.

35 "He was the lamp that was burning and was shining and you were willing to rejoice for a while in his light.

36 "But the testimony which I have is greater than *the testimony of* John; for the works which the Father has given Me to accomplish—the very works that I do—testify about Me, that the Father has sent Me.

37 "And the Father who sent Me, He has testified of Me. You have neither heard His voice at any time nor seen His form.

38 "You do not have His word abiding in you, for you do not believe Him whom He sent.

39 "You search the Scriptures because you think that in them you have eternal life; it is these that testify about Me;

40 and you are unwilling to come to Me so that you may have life.

41 "I do not receive glory from men;

42 but I know you, that you do not have the love of God in yourselves.

43 "I have come in My Father's name, and you do not receive Me; if another comes in his own name, you will receive him.

44 "How can you believe, when you receive glory from one another and you do not seek the glory that is from the *one and only* God?

45 "Do not think that I will accuse you before the Father; the one who accuses you is Moses, in whom you have set your hope.

46 "For if you believed Moses, you would believe Me, for he wrote about Me.

47 "But if you do not believe his writings, how will you believe My words?"

Chapter 6

1 After these things Jesus went away to the other side of the Sea of Galilee (or Tiberias).

2 A large crowd followed Him, because they saw the signs which He was performing on those who were sick.

3 Then Jesus went up on the mountain, and there He sat down with His disciples.

4 Now the Passover, the feast of the Jews, was near.

5 Therefore Jesus, lifting up His eyes and seeing that a large crowd was coming to Him, said to Philip, "Where are we to buy bread, so that these may eat?"

6 This He was saying to test him, for He Himself knew what He was intending to do.

7 Philip answered Him, "Two hundred denarii worth of bread is not sufficient for them, for everyone to receive a little."

8 One of His disciples, Andrew, Simon Peter's brother, said to Him,

9 "There is a lad here who has five barley loaves and two fish, but what are these for so many people?"

10 Jesus said, "Have the people sit down." Now there was much grass in the place. So the men sat down, in number about five thousand.

11 Jesus then took the loaves, and having given thanks, He distributed to those who were seated; likewise also of the fish as much as they wanted.

12 When they were filled, He said to His disciples, "Gather up the leftover fragments so that nothing will be lost."

13 So they gathered them up, and filled twelve baskets with fragments from the five barley loaves which were left over by those who had eaten.

14 Therefore when the people saw the sign which He had performed, they said, "This is truly the Prophet who is to come into the world."

15 So Jesus, perceiving that they were intending to come and take Him by force to make Him king, withdrew again to the mountain by Himself alone.

16 Now when evening came, His disciples went down to the sea, 17 and after getting into a boat, they *started to* cross the sea to Capernaum. It had already become dark, and Jesus had not yet come to them.

18 The sea *began* to be stirred up because a strong wind was blowing.

19 Then, when they had rowed about three or four miles, they saw Jesus walking on the sea and drawing near to the boat; and they were frightened.

20 But He said to them, "It is I; do not be afraid."

21 So they were willing to receive Him into the boat, and immediately the boat was at the land to which they were going.

22 The next day the crowd that stood on the other side of the sea saw that there was no other small boat there, except one, and that Jesus had not entered with His disciples into the boat, but *that* His disciples had gone away alone.

23 There came other small boats from Tiberias near to the place where they ate the bread after the Lord had given thanks.

24 So when the crowd saw that Jesus was not there, nor His disciples, they themselves got into the small boats, and came to Capernaum seeking Jesus.

25 When they found Him on the other side of the sea, they said to Him, "Rabbi, when did You get here?"

26 Jesus answered them and said, "Truly, truly, I say to you, you seek Me, not because you saw signs, but because you ate of the loaves and were filled.

27 "Do not work for the food which perishes, but for the food which endures to eternal life, which the Son of Man will give to you, for on Him the Father, God, has set His seal."

28 Therefore they said to Him, "What shall we do, so that we may work the works of God?"

29 Jesus answered and said to them, "This is the work of God, that you believe in Him whom He has sent."

30 So they said to Him, "What then do You do for a sign, so that we may see, and believe You? What work do You perform?

31 "Our fathers ate the manna in the wilderness; as it is written, 'HE GAVE THEM BREAD OUT OF HEAVEN TO EAT.'"

32 Jesus then said to them, "Truly, truly, I say to you, it is not Moses who has given you the bread out of heaven, but it is My Father who gives you the true bread out of heaven.

33 "For the bread of God is that which comes down out of heaven, and gives life to the world."

34 Then they said to Him, "Lord, always give us this bread."

35 Jesus said to them, "I am the bread of life; he who comes to Me will not hunger, and he who believes in Me will never thirst.

36 "But I said to you that you have seen Me, and yet do not believe.

37 "All that the Father gives Me will come to Me, and the one who comes to Me I will certainly not cast out.

38 "For I have come down from heaven, not to do My own will, but the will of Him who sent Me.

39 "This is the will of Him who sent Me, that of all that He has given Me I lose nothing, but raise it up on the last day.

40 "For this is the will of My Father, that everyone who beholds the Son and believes in Him will have eternal life, and I Myself will raise him up on the last day."

41 Therefore the Jews were grumbling about Him, because He said, "I am the bread that came down out of heaven."

42 They were saying, "Is not this Jesus, the son of Joseph, whose father and mother we know? How does He now say, 'I have come down out of heaven'?"

43 Jesus answered and said to them, "Do not grumble among yourselves.

44 "No one can come to Me unless the Father who sent Me draws him; and I will raise him up on the last day.

45 "It is written in the prophets, 'AND THEY SHALL ALL BE TAUGHT OF GOD.' Everyone who has heard and learned from the Father, comes to Me.

46 "Not that anyone has seen the Father, except the One who is from God; He has seen the Father.

47 "Truly, truly, I say to you, he who believes has eternal life.

48 "I am the bread of life.

49 "Your fathers ate the manna in the wilderness, and they died.

50 "This is the bread which comes down out of heaven, so that one may eat of it and not die.

51 "I am the living bread that came down out of heaven; if anyone eats of this bread, he will live forever; and the bread also which I will give for the life of the world is My flesh."

52 Then the Jews *began* to argue with one another, saying, "How can this man give us *His* flesh to eat?"

53 So Jesus said to them, "Truly, truly, I say to you, unless you eat the flesh of the Son of Man and drink His blood, you have no life in yourselves.

54 "He who eats My flesh and drinks My blood has eternal life, and I will raise him up on the last day.

55 "For My flesh is true food, and My blood is true drink.

56 "He who eats My flesh and drinks My blood abides in Me, and I in him.

57 "As the living Father sent Me, and I live because of the Father, so he who eats Me, he also will live because of Me.

58 "This is the bread which came down out of heaven; not as the fathers ate and died; he who eats this bread will live forever."

59 These things He said in the synagogue as He taught in Capernaum.

60 Therefore many of His disciples, when they heard *this* said, "This is a difficult statement; who can listen to it?"

61 But Jesus, conscious that His disciples grumbled at this, said to them, "Does this cause you to stumble?

62 "*What* then if you see the Son of Man ascending to where He was before?

63 "It is the Spirit who gives life; the flesh profits nothing; the words that I have spoken to you are spirit and are life.

64 "But there are some of you who do not believe." For Jesus knew from the beginning who they were who did not believe, and who it was that would betray Him.

65 And He was saying, "For this reason I have said to you, that no one can come to Me unless it has been granted him from the Father."

66 As a result of this many of His disciples withdrew and were not walking with Him anymore.

67 So Jesus said to the twelve, "You do not want to go away also, do you?"

68 Simon Peter answered Him, "Lord, to whom shall we go? You have words of eternal life.

69 "We have believed and have come to know that You are the Holy One of God."

70 Jesus answered them, "Did I Myself not choose you, the twelve, and *yet* one of you is a devil?"

71 Now He meant Judas *the son* of Simon Iscariot, for he, one of the twelve, was going to betray Him.

Chapter 7

1 After these things Jesus was walking in Galilee, for He was unwilling to walk in Judea because the Jews were seeking to kill Him.

2 Now the feast of the Jews, the Feast of Booths, was near.

3 Therefore His brothers said to Him, "Leave here and go into Judea, so that Your disciples also may see Your works which You are doing.

4 "For no one does anything in secret when he himself seeks to be *known* publicly. If You do these things, show Yourself to the world."

5 For not even His brothers were believing in Him.

6 So Jesus said to them, "My time is not yet here, but your time is always opportune.

7 "The world cannot hate you, but it hates Me because I testify of it, that its deeds are evil.

8 "Go up to the feast yourselves; I do not go up to this feast because My time has not yet fully come."

9 Having said these things to them, He stayed in Galilee.

10 But when His brothers had gone up to the feast, then He Himself also went up, not publicly, but as if, in secret.

11 So the Jews were seeking Him at the feast and were saying, "Where is He?"

12 There was much grumbling among the crowds concerning Him; some were saying, "He is a good man"; others were saying, "No, on the contrary, He leads the people astray."

13 Yet no one was speaking openly of Him for fear of the Jews.

14 But when it was now the midst of the feast Jesus went up into the temple, and *began to* teach.

15 The Jews then were astonished, saying, "How has this man become learned, having never been educated?"

16 So Jesus answered them and said, "My teaching is not Mine, but His who sent Me.

17 "If anyone is willing to do His will, he will know of the teaching, whether it is of God or *whether* I speak from Myself.

18 "He who speaks from himself seeks his own glory; but He who is seeking the glory of the One who sent Him, He is true, and there is no unrighteousness in Him.

19 "Did not Moses give you the Law, and *yet* none of you carries out the Law? Why do you seek to kill Me?"

20 The crowd answered, "You have a demon! Who seeks to kill You?"

21 Jesus answered them, "I did one deed, and you all marvel.

22 "For this reason Moses has given you circumcision (not because it is from Moses, but from the fathers), and on *the* Sabbath you circumcise a man.

23 "If a man receives circumcision on *the* Sabbath so that the Law of Moses will not be broken, are you angry with Me because I made an entire man well on *the* Sabbath?

24 "Do not judge according to appearance, but judge with righteous judgment."

25 So some of the people of Jerusalem were saying, "Is this not the man whom they are seeking to kill?

26 "Look, He is speaking publicly, and they are saying nothing to Him. The rulers do not really know that this is the Christ, do they?

27 "However, we know where this man is from; but whenever the Christ may come, no one knows where He is from."

28 Then Jesus cried out in the temple, teaching and saying, "You both know Me and know where I am from; and I have not come of Myself, but He who sent Me is true, whom you do not know.

29 "I know Him, because I am from Him, and He sent Me."

30 So they were seeking to seize Him; and no man laid his hand on Him, because His hour had not yet come.

31 But many of the crowd believed in Him; and they were saying, "When the Christ comes, He will not perform more signs than those which this man has, will He?"

32 The Pharisees heard the crowd muttering these things about Him, and the chief priests and the Pharisees sent officers to seize Him.

33 Therefore Jesus said, "For a little while longer I am with you, then I go to Him who sent Me.

34 "You will seek Me, and will not find Me; and where I am, you cannot come."

35 The Jews then said to one another, "Where does this man intend to go that we will not find Him? He is not intending to go to the Dispersion among the Greeks, and teach the Greeks, is He?

36 "What is this statement that He said, 'You will seek Me, and will not find Me; and where I am, you cannot come'?"

37 Now on the last day, the great *day* of the feast, Jesus stood and cried out, saying, "If anyone is thirsty, let him come to Me and drink.

38 "He who believes in Me, as the Scripture said, 'From his innermost being will flow rivers of living water.'"

39 But this He spoke of the Spirit, whom those who believed in Him were to receive; for the Spirit was not yet *given*, because Jesus was not yet glorified.

40 *Some* of the people therefore, when they heard these words, were saying, "This certainly is the Prophet."

41 Others were saying, "This is the Christ." Still others were saying, "Surely the Christ is not going to come from Galilee, is He?

42 "Has not the Scripture said that the Christ comes from the descendants of David, and from Bethlehem, the village where David was?"

43 So a division occurred in the crowd because of Him.

44 Some of them wanted to seize Him, but no one laid hands on Him.

45 The officers then came to the chief priests and Pharisees, and they said to them, "Why did you not bring Him?"

46 The officers answered, "Never has a man spoken the way this man speaks."

47 The Pharisees then answered them, "You have not also been led astray, have you?

48 "No one of the rulers or Pharisees has believed in Him, has he?

49 "But this crowd which does not know the Law is accursed."

50 Nicodemus (he who came to Him before, being one of them) said to them,

51 "Our Law does not judge a man unless it first hears from him and knows what he is doing, does it?"

52 They answered him, "You are not also from Galilee, are you? Search, and see that no prophet arises out of Galilee."

53 [Everyone went to his home.

Chapter 8

1 But Jesus went to the Mount of Olives.

2 Early in the morning He came again into the temple, and all the people were coming to Him; and He sat down and *began* to teach them.

3 The scribes and the Pharisees brought a woman caught in adultery, and having set her in the center *of the court,*

4 they said to Him, "Teacher, this woman has been caught in adultery, in the very act.

5 "Now in the Law Moses commanded us to stone such women; what then do You say?"

6 They were saying this, testing Him, so that they might have grounds for accusing Him. But Jesus stooped down and with His finger wrote on the ground.

7 But when they persisted in asking Him, He straightened up, and said to them, "He who is without sin among you, let him *be the* first to throw a stone at her."

8 Again He stooped down and wrote on the ground.

9 When they heard it, they *began* to go out one by one, beginning with the older ones, and He was left alone, and the woman, where she was, in the center *of the court.*

10 Straightening up, Jesus said to her, "Woman, where are they? Did no one condemn you?"

11 She said, "No one, Lord." And Jesus said, "I do not condemn you, either. Go. From now on sin no more."]

12 Then Jesus again spoke to them, saying, "I am the Light of the world; he who follows Me will not walk in the darkness, but will have the Light of life."

13 So the Pharisees said to Him, "You are testifying about Yourself; Your testimony is not true."

14 Jesus answered and said to them, "Even if I testify about Myself, My testimony is true, for I know where I came from and where I am going; but you do not know where I come from or where I am going.

15 "You judge according to the flesh; I am not judging anyone.

16 "But even if I do judge, My judgment is true; for I am not alone *in it,* but I and the Father who sent Me.

17 "Even in your law it has been written that the testimony of two men is true.

18 "I am He who testifies about Myself, and the Father who sent Me testifies about Me."

19 So they were saying to Him, "Where is Your Father?" Jesus answered, "You know neither Me nor My Father; if you knew Me, you would know My Father also."

20 These words He spoke in the treasury, as He taught in the temple; and no one seized Him, because His hour had not yet come.

21 Then He said again to them, "I go away, and you will seek Me, and will die in your sin; where I am going, you cannot come."

22 So the Jews were saying, "Surely He will not kill Himself, will He, since He says, 'Where I am going, you cannot come'?"

23 And He was saying to them, "You are from below, I am from above; you are of this world, I am not of this world.

24 "Therefore I said to you that you will die in your sins; for unless you believe that I am *He*, you will die in your sins."

25 So they were saying to Him, "Who are You?" Jesus said to them, "What have I been saying to you *from* the beginning?

26 "I have many things to speak and to judge concerning you, but He who sent Me is true; and the things which I heard from Him, these I speak to the world."

27 They did not realize that He had been speaking to them about the Father.

28 So Jesus said, "When you lift up the Son of Man, then you will know that I am *He*, and I do nothing on My own initiative, but I speak these things as the Father taught Me.

29 "And He who sent Me is with Me; He has not left Me alone, for I always do the things that are pleasing to Him."

30 As He spoke these things, many came to believe in Him.

31 So Jesus was saying to those Jews who had believed Him, "If you continue in My word, *then* you are truly disciples of Mine;

32 and you will know the truth, and the truth will make you free."

33 They answered Him, "We are Abraham's descendants and have never yet been enslaved to anyone; how is it that You say, 'You will become free'?"

34 Jesus answered them, "Truly, truly, I say to you, everyone who commits sin is the slave of sin.

35 "The slave does not remain in the house forever; the son does remain forever.

36 "So if the Son makes you free, you will be free indeed.

37 "I know that you are Abraham's descendants; yet you seek to kill Me, because My word has no place in you.

38 "I speak the things which I have seen with My Father; therefore you also do the things which you heard from *your* father."

39 They answered and said to Him, "Abraham is our father." Jesus said to them, "If you are Abraham's children, do the deeds of Abraham.

40 "But as it is, you are seeking to kill Me, a man who has told you the truth, which I heard from God; this Abraham did not do.

41 "You are doing the deeds of your father." They said to Him, "We were not born of fornication; we have one Father: God."

42 Jesus said to them, "If God were your Father, you would love Me, for I proceeded forth and have come from God, for I have not even come on My own initiative, but He sent Me.

43 "Why do you not understand what I am saying? *It is* because you cannot hear My word.

44 "You are of *your* father the devil, and you want to do the desires of your father. He was a murderer from the beginning, and does not stand in the truth because there is no truth in him. Whenever he speaks a lie, he speaks from his own *nature*, for he is a liar and the father of lies.

45 "But because I speak the truth, you do not believe Me.

46 "Which one of you convicts Me of sin? If I speak truth, why do you not believe Me?

47 "He who is of God hears the words of God; for this reason you do not hear *them*, because you are not of God."

48 The Jews answered and said to Him, "Do we not say rightly that You are a Samaritan and have a demon?"

49 Jesus answered, "I do not have a demon; but I honor My Father, and you dishonor Me.

50 "But I do not seek My glory; there is One who seeks and judges.

51 "Truly, truly, I say to you, if anyone keeps My word he will never see death."

52 The Jews said to Him, "Now we know that You have a demon. Abraham died, and the prophets *also*; and You say, 'If anyone keeps My word, he will never taste of death.'

53 "Surely You are not greater than our father Abraham, who died? The prophets died too; whom do You make Yourself out *to be?*"

54 Jesus answered, "If I glorify Myself, My glory is nothing; it is My Father who glorifies Me, of whom you say, 'He is our God';

55 and you have not come to know Him, but I know Him; and if I say that I do not know Him, I will be a liar like you, but I do know Him and keep His word.

56 "Your father Abraham rejoiced to see My day, and he saw *it* and was glad."

57 So the Jews said to Him, "You are not yet fifty years old, and have You seen Abraham?"

58 Jesus said to them, "Truly, truly, I say to you, before Abraham was born, I am."

59 Therefore they picked up stones to throw at Him, but Jesus hid Himself and went out of the temple.

Chapter 9

1 As He passed by, He saw a man blind from birth.

2 And His disciples asked Him, "Rabbi, who sinned, this man or his parents, that he would be born blind?"

3 Jesus answered, "*It was* neither *that* this man sinned, nor his parents; but *it was* so that the works of God might be displayed in him.

4 "We must work the works of Him who sent Me as long as it is day; night is coming when no one can work.

5 "While I am in the world, I am the Light of the world."

6 When He had said this, He spat on the ground, and made clay of the spittle, and applied the clay to his eyes,

7 and said to him, "Go, wash in the pool of Siloam" (which is translated, Sent). So he went away and washed, and came *back* seeing.

8 Therefore the neighbors, and those who previously saw him as a beggar, were saying, "Is not this the one who used to sit and beg?"

9 Others were saying, "This is he," *still* others were saying, "No, but he is like him." He kept saying, "I am the one."

10 So they were saying to him, "How then were your eyes opened?"

11 He answered, "The man who is called Jesus made clay, and anointed my eyes, and said to me, 'Go to Siloam and wash'; so I went away and washed, and I received sight."

12 They said to him, "Where is He?" He said, "I do not know."

13 They brought to the Pharisees the man who was formerly blind.

14 Now it was a Sabbath on the day when Jesus made the clay and opened his eyes.

15 Then the Pharisees also were asking him again how he received his sight. And he said to them, "He applied clay to my eyes, and I washed, and I see."

16 Therefore some of the Pharisees were saying, "This man is not from God, because He does not keep the Sabbath." But others were saying, "How can a man who is a sinner perform such signs?" And there was a division among them.

17 So they said to the blind man again, "What do you say about Him, since He opened your eyes?" And he said, "He is a prophet."

18 The Jews then did not believe it of him, that he had been blind and had received sight, until they called the parents of the very one who had received his sight,

19 and questioned them, saying, "Is this your son, who you say was born blind? Then how does he now see?"

20 His parents answered them and said, "We know that this is our son, and that he was born blind;

21 but how he now sees, we do not know; or who opened his eyes, we do not know. Ask him; he is of age, he will speak for himself."

22 His parents said this because they were afraid of the Jews; for the Jews had already agreed that if anyone confessed Him to be Christ, he was to be put out of the synagogue.

23 For this reason his parents said, "He is of age; ask him."

24 So a second time they called the man who had been blind, and said to him, "Give glory to God; we know that this man is a sinner."

25 He then answered, "Whether He is a sinner, I do not know; one thing I do know, that though I was blind, now I see."

26 So they said to him, "What did He do to you? How did He open your eyes?"

27 He answered them, "I told you already and you did not listen; why do you want to hear it again? You do not want to become His disciples too, do you?"

28 They reviled him and said, "You are His disciple, but we are disciples of Moses.

29 "We know that God has spoken to Moses, but as for this man, we do not know where He is from."

30 The man answered and said to them, "Well, here is an amazing thing, that you do not know where He is from, and *yet* He opened my eyes.

31 "We know that God does not hear sinners; but if anyone is God-fearing and does His will, He hears him.

32 "Since the beginning of time it has never been heard that anyone opened the eyes of a person born blind.

33 "If this man were not from God, He could do nothing."

34 They answered him, "You were born entirely in sins, and are you teaching us?" So they put him out.

35 Jesus heard that they had put him out, and finding him, He said, "Do you believe in the Son of Man?"

36 He answered, "Who is He, Lord, that I may believe in Him?"

37 Jesus said to him, "You have both seen Him, and He is the one who is talking with you."

38 And he said, "Lord, I believe." And he worshiped Him.

39 And Jesus said, "For judgment I came into this world, so that those who do not see may see, and that those who see may become blind."

40 Those of the Pharisees who were with Him heard these things and said to Him, "We are not blind too, are we?"

41 Jesus said to them, "If you were blind, you would have no sin; but since you say, 'We see,' your sin remains.

Chapter 10

1 "Truly, truly, I say to you, he who does not enter by the door into the fold of the sheep, but climbs up some other way, he is a thief and a robber.

2 "But he who enters by the door is a shepherd of the sheep.

3 "To him the doorkeeper opens, and the sheep hear his voice, and he calls his own sheep by name and leads them out.

4 "When he puts forth all his own, he goes ahead of them, and the sheep follow him because they know his voice.

5 "A stranger they simply will not follow, but will flee from him, because they do not know the voice of strangers."

6 This figure of speech Jesus spoke to them, but they did not understand what those things were which He had been saying to them.

7 So Jesus said to them again, "Truly, truly, I say to you, I am the door of the sheep.

8 "All who came before Me are thieves and robbers, but the sheep did not hear them.

9 "I am the door; if anyone enters through Me, he will be saved, and will go in and out and find pasture.

10 "The thief comes only to steal and kill and destroy; I came that they may have life, and have *it* abundantly.

11 "I am the good shepherd; the good shepherd lays down His life for the sheep.

12 "He who is a hired hand, and not a shepherd, who is not the owner of the sheep, sees the wolf coming, and leaves the sheep and flees, and the wolf snatches them and scatters *them*.

13 "*He flees* because he is a hired hand and is not concerned about the sheep.

14 "I am the good shepherd, and I know My own and My own know Me,

15 even as the Father knows Me and I know the Father; and I lay down My life for the sheep.

16 "I have other sheep, which are not of this fold; I must bring them also, and they will hear My voice; and they will become one flock *with* one shepherd.

17 "For this reason the Father loves Me, because I lay down My life so that I may take it again.

18 "No one has taken it away from Me, but I lay it down on My own initiative. I have authority to lay it down, and I have authority to take it up again. This commandment I received from My Father."

19 A division occurred again among the Jews because of these words.

20 Many of them were saying, "He has a demon and is insane. Why do you listen to Him?"

21 Others were saying, "These are not the sayings of one demon-possessed. A demon cannot open the eyes of the blind, can he?"

22 At that time the Feast of the Dedication took place at Jerusalem;

23 it was winter, and Jesus was walking in the temple in the portico of Solomon.

24 The Jews then gathered around Him, and were saying to Him, "How long will You keep us in suspense? If You are the Christ, tell us plainly."

25 Jesus answered them, "I told you, and you do not believe; the works that I do in My Father's name, these testify of Me.

26 "But you do not believe because you are not of My sheep.

27 "My sheep hear My voice, and I know them, and they follow Me;

28 and I give eternal life to them, and they will never perish; and no one will snatch them out of My hand.

29 "My Father, who has given *them* to Me, is greater than all; and no one is able to snatch *them* out of the Father's hand.

30 "I and the Father are one."

31 The Jews picked up stones again to stone Him.

32 Jesus answered them, "I showed you many good works from the Father; for which of them are you stoning Me?"

33 The Jews answered Him, "For a good work we do not stone You, but for blasphemy; and because You, being a man, make Yourself out *to be* God."

34 Jesus answered them, "Has it not been written in your Law, 'I SAID, YOU ARE GODS'?

35 "If he called them gods, to whom the word of God came (and the Scripture cannot be broken),

36 do you say of Him, whom the Father sanctified and sent into the world, 'You are blaspheming,' because I said, 'I am the Son of God'?

37 "If I do not do the works of My Father, do not believe Me;

38 but if I do them, though you do not believe Me, believe the works, so that you may know and understand that the Father is in Me, and I in the Father."

39 Therefore they were seeking again to seize Him, and He eluded their grasp.

40 And He went away again beyond the Jordan to the place where John was first baptizing, and He was staying there.

41 Many came to Him and were saying, "While John performed no sign, yet everything John said about this man was true."

42 Many believed in Him there.

Chapter 11

1 Now a certain man was sick, Lazarus of Bethany, the village of Mary and her sister Martha.

2 It was the Mary who anointed the Lord with ointment, and wiped His feet with her hair, whose brother Lazarus was sick.

3 So the sisters sent *word* to Him, saying, "Lord, behold, he whom You love is sick."

4 But when Jesus heard *this*, He said, "This sickness is not to end in death, but for the glory of God, so that the Son of God may be glorified by it."

5 Now Jesus loved Martha and her sister and Lazarus.

6 So when He heard that he was sick, He then stayed two days *longer* in the place where He was.

7 Then after this He said to the disciples, "Let us go to Judea again."

8 The disciples said to Him, "Rabbi, the Jews were just now seeking to stone You, and are You going there again?"

9 Jesus answered, "Are there not twelve hours in the day? If anyone walks in the day, he does not stumble, because he sees the light of this world.

10 "But if anyone walks in the night, he stumbles, because the light is not in him."

11 This He said, and after that He said to them, "Our friend Lazarus has fallen asleep; but I go, so that I may awaken him out of sleep."

12 The disciples then said to Him, "Lord, if he has fallen asleep, he will recover."

13 Now Jesus had spoken of his death, but they thought that He was speaking of literal sleep.

14 So Jesus then said to them plainly, "Lazarus is dead,

15 and I am glad for your sakes that I was not there, so that you may believe; but let us go to him."

16 Therefore Thomas, who is called Didymus, said to *his* fellow disciples, "Let us also go, so that we may die with Him."

17 So when Jesus came, He found that he had already been in the tomb four days.

18 Now Bethany was near Jerusalem, about two miles off;

19 and many of the Jews had come to Martha and Mary, to console them concerning *their* brother.

20 Martha therefore, when she heard that Jesus was coming, went to meet Him, but Mary stayed at the house.

21 Martha then said to Jesus, "Lord, if You had been here, my brother would not have died.

22 "Even now I know that whatever You ask of God, God will give You."

23 Jesus said to her, "Your brother will rise again."

24 Martha said to Him, "I know that he will rise again in the resurrection on the last day."

25 Jesus said to her, "I am the resurrection and the life; he who believes in Me will live even if he dies,

26 and everyone who lives and believes in Me will never die. Do you believe this?"

27 She said to Him, "Yes, Lord; I have believed that You are the Christ, the Son of God, *even* He who comes into the world."

28 When she had said this, she went away and called Mary her sister, saying secretly, "The Teacher is here and is calling for you."

29 And when she heard it, she got up quickly and was coming to Him.

30 Now Jesus had not yet come into the village, but was still in the place where Martha met Him.

31 Then the Jews who were with her in the house, and consoling her, when they saw that Mary got up quickly and went out, they followed her, supposing that she was going to the tomb to weep there.

32 Therefore, when Mary came where Jesus was, she saw Him, and fell at His feet, saying to Him, "Lord, if You had been here, my brother would not have died."

33 When Jesus therefore saw her weeping, and the Jews who came with her *also* weeping, He was deeply moved in spirit and was troubled,

34 and said, "Where have you laid him?" They said to Him, "Lord, come and see."

35 Jesus wept.

36 So the Jews were saying, "See how He loved him!"

37 But some of them said, "Could not this man, who opened the eyes of the blind man, have kept this man also from dying?"

38 So Jesus, again being deeply moved within, came to the tomb. Now it was a cave, and a stone was lying against it.

39 Jesus said, "Remove the stone." Martha, the sister of the deceased, said to Him, "Lord, by this time there will be a stench, for he has been *dead* four days."

40 Jesus said to her, "Did I not say to you that if you believe, you will see the glory of God?"

41 So they removed the stone. Then Jesus raised His eyes, and said, "Father, I thank You that You have heard Me.

42 "I knew that You always hear Me; but because of the people standing around I said it, so that they may believe that You sent Me."

43 When He had said these things, He cried out with a loud voice, "Lazarus, come forth."

44 The man who had died came forth, bound hand and foot with wrappings, and his face was wrapped around with a cloth. Jesus said to them, "Unbind him, and let him go."

45 Therefore many of the Jews who came to Mary, and saw what He had done, believed in Him.

46 But some of them went to the Pharisees and told them the things which Jesus had done.

47 Therefore the chief priests and the Pharisees convened a council, and were saying, "What are we doing? For this man is performing many signs.

48 "If we let Him *go on* like this, all men will believe in Him, and the Romans will come and take away both our place and our nation."

49 But one of them, Caiaphas, who was high priest that year, said to them, "You know nothing at all,

50 nor do you take into account that it is expedient for you that one man die for the people, and that the whole nation not perish."

51 Now he did not say this on his own initiative, but being high priest that year, he prophesied that Jesus was going to die for the nation,

52 and not for the nation only, but in order that He might also gather together into one the children of God who are scattered abroad.

53 So from that day on they planned together to kill Him.

54 Therefore Jesus no longer continued to walk publicly among the Jews, but went away from there to the country near the wilderness, into a city called Ephraim; and there He stayed with the disciples.

55 Now the Passover of the Jews was near, and many went up to Jerusalem out of the country before the Passover to purify themselves.

56 So they were seeking for Jesus, and were saying to one another as they stood in the temple, "What do you think; that He will not come to the feast at all?"

57 Now the chief priests and the Pharisees had given orders that if anyone knew where He was, he was to report it, so that they might seize Him.

Chapter 12

1 Jesus, therefore, six days before the Passover, came to Bethany where Lazarus was, whom Jesus had raised from the dead.

2 So they made Him a supper there, and Martha was serving; but Lazarus was one of those reclining *at the table* with Him.

3 Mary then took a pound of very costly perfume of pure nard, and anointed the feet of Jesus and wiped His feet with her hair; and the house was filled with the fragrance of the perfume.

4 But Judas Iscariot, one of His disciples, who was intending to betray Him, said,

5 "Why was this perfume not sold for three hundred denarii and given to poor *people?*"

6 Now he said this, not because he was concerned about the poor, but because he was a thief, and as he had the money box, he used to pilfer what was put into it.

7 Therefore Jesus said, "Let her alone, so that she may keep it for the day of My burial.

8 "For you always have the poor with you, but you do not always have Me."

9 The large crowd of the Jews then learned that He was there; and they came, not for Jesus' sake only, but that they might also see Lazarus, whom He raised from the dead.

10 But the chief priests planned to put Lazarus to death also;

11 because on account of him many of the Jews were going away and were believing in Jesus.

12 On the next day the large crowd who had come to the feast, when they heard that Jesus was coming to Jerusalem,

13 took the branches of the palm trees and went out to meet Him, and *began* to shout, "Hosanna! BLESSED IS HE WHO COMES IN THE NAME OF THE LORD, even the King of Israel."

14 Jesus, finding a young donkey, sat on it; as it is written,

15 "FEAR NOT, DAUGHTER OF ZION; BEHOLD, YOUR KING IS COMING, SEATED ON A DONKEY'S COLT."

16 These things His disciples did not understand at the first; but when Jesus was glorified, then they remembered that these things were written of Him, and that they had done these things to Him.

17 So the people, who were with Him when He called Lazarus out of the tomb and raised him from the dead, continued to testify *about Him*.

18 For this reason also the people went and met Him, because they heard that He had performed this sign.

19 So the Pharisees said to one another, "You see that you are not doing any good; look, the world has gone after Him."

20 Now there were some Greeks among those who were going up to worship at the feast;

21 these then came to Philip, who was from Bethsaida of Galilee, and *began to* ask him, saying, "Sir, we wish to see Jesus."

22 Philip came and told Andrew; Andrew and Philip came and told Jesus.

23 And Jesus answered them, saying, "The hour has come for the Son of Man to be glorified.

24 "Truly, truly, I say to you, unless a grain of wheat falls into the earth and dies, it remains alone; but if it dies, it bears much fruit.

25 "He who loves his life loses it, and he who hates his life in this world will keep it to life eternal.

26 "If anyone serves Me, he must follow Me; and where I am, there My servant will be also; if anyone serves Me, the Father will honor him.

27 "Now My soul has become troubled; and what shall I say, 'Father, save Me from this hour'? But for this purpose I came to this hour.

28 "Father, glorify Your name." Then a voice came out of heaven: "I have both glorified it, and will glorify it again."

29 So the crowd *of people* who stood by and heard it were saying that it had thundered; others were saying, "An angel has spoken to Him."

30 Jesus answered and said, "This voice has not come for My sake, but for your sakes.

31 "Now judgment is upon this world; now the ruler of this world will be cast out.

32 "And I, if I am lifted up from the earth, will draw all men to Myself."

33 But He was saying this to indicate the kind of death by which He was to die.

34 The crowd then answered Him, "We have heard out of the Law that the Christ is to remain forever; and how can You say, 'The Son of Man must be lifted up'? Who is this Son of Man?"

35 So Jesus said to them, "For a little while longer the Light is among you. Walk while you have the Light, so that darkness will not overtake you; he who walks in the darkness does not know where he goes.

36 "While you have the Light, believe in the Light, so that you may become sons of Light."

These things Jesus spoke, and He went away and hid Himself from them.

37 But though He had performed so many signs before them, *yet* they were not believing in Him.

38 *This was* to fulfill the word of Isaiah the prophet which he spoke: "LORD, WHO HAS BELIEVED OUR REPORT? AND TO WHOM HAS THE ARM OF THE LORD BEEN REVEALED?"

39 For this reason they could not believe, for Isaiah said again,

40 "HE HAS BLINDED THEIR EYES AND HE HARDENED THEIR HEART, SO THAT THEY WOULD NOT SEE WITH THEIR EYES AND PERCEIVE WITH THEIR HEART, AND BE CONVERTED AND I HEAL THEM."

41 These things Isaiah said because he saw His glory, and he spoke of Him.

42 Nevertheless many even of the rulers believed in Him, but because of the Pharisees they were not confessing *Him*, for fear that they would be put out of the synagogue;

43 for they loved the approval of men rather than the approval of God.

44 And Jesus cried out and said, "He who believes in Me, does not believe in Me but in Him who sent Me.

45 "He who sees Me sees the One who sent Me.

46 "I have come *as* Light into the world, so that everyone who believes in Me will not remain in darkness.

47 "If anyone hears My sayings and does not keep them, I do not judge him; for I did not come to judge the world, but to save the world.

48 "He who rejects Me and does not receive My sayings, has one who judges him; the word I spoke is what will judge him at the last day.

49 "For I did not speak on My own initiative, but the Father Himself who sent Me has given Me a commandment *as to* what to say and what to speak.

50 "I know that His commandment is eternal life; therefore the things I speak, I speak just as the Father has told Me."

Chapter 13

1 Now before the Feast of the Passover, Jesus knowing that His hour had come that He would depart out of this world to the Father, having loved His own who were in the world, He loved them to the end.

2 During supper, the devil having already put into the heart of Judas Iscariot, *the son* of Simon, to betray Him,

3 *Jesus*, knowing that the Father had given all things into His hands, and that He had come forth from God and was going back to God,

4 got up from supper, and laid aside His garments; and taking a towel, He girded Himself.

5 Then He poured water into the basin, and began to wash the disciples' feet and to wipe them with the towel with which He was girded.

6 So He came to Simon Peter. He said to Him, "Lord, do You wash my feet?"

7 Jesus answered and said to him, "What I do you do not realize now, but you will understand hereafter."

8 Peter said to Him, "Never shall You wash my feet!" Jesus answered him, "If I do not wash you, you have no part with Me."

9 Simon Peter said to Him, "Lord, *then wash* not only my feet, but also my hands and my head."

10 Jesus said to him, "He who has bathed needs only to wash his feet, but is completely clean; and you are clean, but not all *of you.*"

11 For He knew the one who was betraying Him; for this reason He said, "Not all of you are clean."

12 So when He had washed their feet, and taken His garments and reclined *at the table* again, He said to them, "Do you know what I have done to you?

13 "You call Me Teacher and Lord; and you are right, for *so* I am.

14 "If I then, the Lord and the Teacher, washed your feet, you also ought to wash one another's feet.

15 "For I gave you an example that you also should do as I did to you.

16 "Truly, truly, I say to you, a slave is not greater than his master, nor *is* one who is sent greater than the one who sent him.

17 "If you know these things, you are blessed if you do them.

18 "I do not speak of all of you. I know the ones I have chosen; but *it is* that the Scripture may be fulfilled, 'HE WHO EATS MY BREAD HAS LIFTED UP HIS HEEL AGAINST ME.'

19 "From now on I am telling you before *it* comes to pass, so that when it does occur, you may believe that I am *He.*

20 "Truly, truly, I say to you, he who receives whomever I send receives Me; and he who receives Me receives Him who sent Me."

21 When Jesus had said this, He became troubled in spirit, and testified and said, "Truly, truly, I say to you, that one of you will betray Me."

22 The disciples *began* looking at one another, at a loss *to know* of which one He was speaking.

23 There was reclining on Jesus' bosom one of His disciples, whom Jesus loved.

24 So Simon Peter gestured to him, and said to him, "Tell *us* who it is of whom He is speaking."

25 He, leaning back thus on Jesus' bosom, said to Him, "Lord, who is it?"

26 Jesus then answered, "That is the one for whom I shall dip the morsel and give it to him." So when He had dipped the morsel, He took and gave it to Judas, *the son* of Simon Iscariot.

27 After the morsel, Satan then entered into him. Therefore Jesus said to him, "What you do, do quickly."

28 Now no one of those reclining *at the table* knew for what purpose He had said this to him.

29 For some were supposing, because Judas had the money box, that Jesus was saying to him, "Buy the things we have need of for the feast"; or else, that he should give something to the poor.

30 So after receiving the morsel he went out immediately; and it was night.

31 Therefore when he had gone out, Jesus said, "Now is the Son of Man glorified, and God is glorified in Him;

32 if God is glorified in Him, God will also glorify Him in Himself, and will glorify Him immediately.

33 "Little children, I am with you a little while longer. You will seek Me; and as I said to the Jews, now I also say to you, 'Where I am going, you cannot come.'

34 "A new commandment I give to you, that you love one another, even as I have loved you, that you also love one another.

35 "By this all men will know that you are My disciples, if you have love for one another."

36 Simon Peter said to Him, "Lord, where are You going?" Jesus answered, "Where I go, you cannot follow Me now; but you will follow later."

37 Peter said to Him, "Lord, why can I not follow You right now? I will lay down my life for You."

38 Jesus answered, "Will you lay down your life for Me? Truly, truly, I say to you, a rooster will not crow until you deny Me three times.

Chapter 14

1 "Do not let your heart be troubled; believe in God, believe also in Me.

2 "In My Father's house are many dwelling places; if it were not so, I would have told you; for I go to prepare a place for you.

3 "If I go and prepare a place for you, I will come again and receive you to Myself, that where I am, *there* you may be also.

4 "And you know the way where I am going."

5 Thomas said to Him, "Lord, we do not know where You are going, how do we know the way?"

6 Jesus said to him, "I am the way, and the truth, and the life; no one comes to the Father but through Me.

7 "If you had known Me, you would have known My Father also; from now on you know Him, and have seen Him."

8 Philip said to Him, "Lord, show us the Father, and it is enough for us."

9 Jesus said to him, "Have I been so long with you, and *yet* you have not come to know Me, Philip? He who has seen Me has seen the Father; how *can* you say, 'Show us the Father'?

10 "Do you not believe that I am in the Father, and the Father is in Me? The words that I say to you I do not speak on My own initiative, but the Father abiding in Me does His works.

11 "Believe Me that I am in the Father and the Father is in Me; otherwise believe because of the works themselves.

12 "Truly, truly, I say to you, he who believes in Me, the works that I do, he will do also; and greater *works* than these he will do; because I go to the Father.

13 "Whatever you ask in My name, that will I do, so that the Father may be glorified in the Son.

14 "If you ask Me anything in My name, I will do *it*.

15 "If you love Me, you will keep My commandments.

16 "I will ask the Father, and He will give you another Helper, that He may be with you forever;

17 *that is* the Spirit of truth, whom the world cannot receive, because it does not see Him or know Him, *but* you know Him because He abides with you and will be in you.

18 "I will not leave you as orphans; I will come to you.

19 "After a little while the world will no longer see Me, but you *will* see Me; because I live, you will live also.

20 "In that day you will know that I am in My Father, and you in Me, and I in you.

21 "He who has My commandments and keeps them is the one who loves Me; and he who loves Me will be loved by My Father, and I will love him and will disclose Myself to him."

22 Judas (not Iscariot) said to Him, "Lord, what then has happened that You are going to disclose Yourself to us and not to the world?"

23 Jesus answered and said to him, "If anyone loves Me, he will keep My word; and My Father will love him, and We will come to him and make Our abode with him.

24 "He who does not love Me does not keep My words; and the word which you hear is not Mine, but the Father's who sent Me.

25 "These things I have spoken to you while abiding with you.

26 "But the Helper, the Holy Spirit, whom the Father will send in My name, He will teach you all things, and bring to your remembrance all that I said to you.

27 "Peace I leave with you; My peace I give to you; not as the world gives do I give to you. Do not let your heart be troubled, nor let it be fearful.

28 "You heard that I said to you, 'I go away, and I will come to you.' If you loved Me, you would have rejoiced because I go to the Father, for the Father is greater than I.

29 "Now I have told you before it happens, so that when it happens, you may believe.

30 "I will not speak much more with you, for the ruler of the world is coming, and he has nothing in Me;

31 but so that the world may know that I love the Father, I do exactly as the Father commanded Me. Get up, let us go from here.

Chapter 15

1 "I am the true vine, and My Father is the vinedresser.

2 "Every branch in Me that does not bear fruit, He takes away; and every *branch* that bears fruit, He prunes it so that it may bear more fruit.

3 "You are already clean because of the word which I have spoken to you.

4 "Abide in Me, and I in you. As the branch cannot bear fruit of itself unless it abides in the vine, so neither *can* you unless you abide in Me.

5 "I am the vine, you are the branches; he who abides in Me and I in him, he bears much fruit, for apart from Me you can do nothing.

6 "If anyone does not abide in Me, he is thrown away as a branch and dries up; and they gather them, and cast them into the fire and they are burned.

7 "If you abide in Me, and My words abide in you, ask whatever you wish, and it will be done for you.

8 "My Father is glorified by this, that you bear much fruit, and *so* prove to be My disciples.

9 "Just as the Father has loved Me, I have also loved you; abide in My love.

10 "If you keep My commandments, you will abide in My love; just as I have kept My Father's commandments and abide in His love.

11 "These things I have spoken to you so that My joy may be in you, and *that* your joy may be made full.

12 "This is My commandment, that you love one another, just as I have loved you.

13 "Greater love has no one than this, that one lay down his life for his friends.

14 "You are My friends if you do what I command you.

15 "No longer do I call you slaves, for the slave does not know what his master is doing; but I have called you friends, for all things that I have heard from My Father I have made known to you.

16 "You did not choose Me but I chose you, and appointed you that you would go and bear fruit, and *that* your fruit would remain, so that whatever you ask of the Father in My name He may give to you.

17 "This I command you, that you love one another.

18 "If the world hates you, you know that it has hated Me before *it hated* you.

19 "If you were of the world, the world would love its own; but because you are not of the world, but I chose you out of the world, because of this the world hates you.

20 "Remember the word that I said to you, 'A slave is not greater than his master.' If they persecuted Me, they will also persecute you; if they kept My word, they will keep yours also.

21 "But all these things they will do to you for My name's sake, because they do not know the One who sent Me.

22 "If I had not come and spoken to them, they would not have sin, but now they have no excuse for their sin.

23 "He who hates Me hates My Father also.

24 "If I had not done among them the works which no one else did, they would not have sin; but now they have both seen and hated Me and My Father as well.

25 "But *they have done this* to fulfill the word that is written in their Law, 'THEY HATED ME WITHOUT A CAUSE.'

26 "When the Helper comes, whom I will send to you from the Father, *that is* the Spirit of truth who proceeds from the Father, He will testify about Me,

27 and you *will* testify also, because you have been with Me from the beginning.

Chapter 16

1 "These things I have spoken to you so that you may be kept from stumbling.

2 "They will make you outcasts from the synagogue, but an hour is coming for everyone who kills you to think that he is offering service to God.

3 "These things they will do because they have not known the Father or Me.

4 "But these things I have spoken to you, so that when their hour comes, you may remember that I told you of them. These things I did not say to you at the beginning, because I was with you.

5 "But now I am going to Him who sent Me; and none of you asks Me, 'Where are You going?'

6 "But because I have said these things to you, sorrow has filled your heart.

7 "But I tell you the truth, it is to your advantage that I go away; for if I do not go away, the Helper will not come to you; but if I go, I will send Him to you.

8 "And He, when He comes, will convict the world concerning sin and righteousness and judgment;

9 concerning sin, because they do not believe in Me;

10 and concerning righteousness, because I go to the Father and you no longer see Me;

11 and concerning judgment, because the ruler of this world has been judged.

12 "I have many more things to say to you, but you cannot bear *them* now.

13 "But when He, the Spirit of truth, comes, He will guide you into all the truth; for He will not speak on His own initiative, but whatever He hears, He will speak; and He will disclose to you what is to come.

14 "He will glorify Me, for He will take of Mine and will disclose *it* to you.

15 "All things that the Father has are Mine; therefore I said that He takes of Mine and will disclose *it* to you.

16 "A little while, and you will no longer see Me; and again a little while, and you will see Me."

17 *Some* of His disciples then said to one another, "What is this thing He is telling us, 'A little while, and you will not see Me; and again a little while, and you will see Me'; and, 'because I go to the Father'?"

18 So they were saying, "What is this that He says, 'A little while'? We do not know what He is talking about."

19 Jesus knew that they wished to question Him, and He said to them, "Are you deliberating together about this, that I said, 'A little while, and you will not see Me, and again a little while, and you will see Me'?

20 "Truly, truly, I say to you, that you will weep and lament, but the world will rejoice; you will grieve, but your grief will be turned into joy.

21 "Whenever a woman is in labor she has pain, because her hour has come; but when she gives birth to the child, she no longer remembers the anguish because of the joy that a child has been born into the world.

22 "Therefore you too have grief now; but I will see you again, and your heart will rejoice, and no one *will* take your joy away from you.

23 "In that day you will not question Me about anything. Truly, truly, I say to you, if you ask the Father for anything in My name, He will give it to you.

24 "Until now you have asked for nothing in My name; ask and you will receive, so that your joy may be made full.

25 "These things I have spoken to you in figurative language; an hour is coming when I will no longer speak to you in figurative language, but will tell you plainly of the Father.

26 "In that day you will ask in My name, and I do not say to you that I will request of the Father on your behalf;

27 for the Father Himself loves you, because you have loved Me and have believed that I came forth from the Father.

28 "I came forth from the Father and have come into the world; I am leaving the world again and going to the Father."

29 His disciples said, "Lo, now You are speaking plainly and are not using a figure of speech.

30 "Now we know that You know all things, and have no need for anyone to question You; by this we believe that You came from God."

31 Jesus answered them, "Do you now believe?

32 "Behold, an hour is coming, and has *already* come, for you to be scattered, each to his own *home*, and to leave Me alone; and *yet* I am not alone, because the Father is with Me.

33 "These things I have spoken to you, so that in Me you may have peace. In the world you have tribulation, but take courage; I have overcome the world."

Chapter 17

1 Jesus spoke these things; and lifting up His eyes to heaven, He said, "Father, the hour has come; glorify Your Son, that the Son may glorify You,

2 even as You gave Him authority over all flesh, that to all whom You have given Him, He may give eternal life.

3 "This is eternal life, that they may know You, the only true God, and Jesus Christ whom You have sent.

4 "I glorified You on the earth, having accomplished the work which You have given Me to do.

5 "Now, Father, glorify Me together with Yourself, with the glory which I had with You before the world was.

6 "I have manifested Your name to the men whom You gave Me out of the world; they were Yours and You gave them to Me, and they have kept Your word.

7 "Now they have come to know that everything You have given Me is from You;

8 for the words which You gave Me I have given to them; and they received *them* and truly understood that I came forth from You, and they believed that You sent Me.

9 "I ask on their behalf; I do not ask on behalf of the world, but of those whom You have given Me; for they are Yours;

10 and all things that are Mine are Yours, and Yours are Mine; and I have been glorified in them.

11 "I am no longer in the world; and *yet* they themselves are in the world, and I come to You. Holy Father, keep them in Your name, *the name* which You have given Me, that they may be one even as We *are*.

12 "While I was with them, I was keeping them in Your name which You have given Me; and I guarded them and not one of them perished but the son of perdition, so that the Scripture would be fulfilled.

13 "But now I come to You; and these things I speak in the world so that they may have My joy made full in themselves.

14 "I have given them Your word; and the world has hated them, because they are not of the world, even as I am not of the world.

15 "I do not ask You to take them out of the world, but to keep them from the evil *one*.

16 "They are not of the world, even as I am not of the world.

17 "Sanctify them in the truth; Your word is truth.

18 "As You sent Me into the world, I also have sent them into the world.

19 "For their sakes I sanctify Myself, that they themselves also may be sanctified in truth.

20 "I do not ask on behalf of these alone, but for those also who believe in Me through their word;

21 that they may all be one; even as You, Father, *are* in Me and I in You, that they also may be in Us, so that the world may believe that You sent Me.

22 "The glory which You have given Me I have given to them, that they may be one, just as We are one;

23 I in them and You in Me, that they may be perfected in unity, so that the world may know that You sent Me, and loved them, even as You have loved Me.

24 "Father, I desire that they also, whom You have given Me, be with Me where I am, so that they may see My glory which You

have given Me, for You loved Me before the foundation of the world.

25 "O righteous Father, although the world has not known You, yet I have known You; and these have known that You sent Me;

26 and I have made Your name known to them, and will make it known, so that the love with which You loved Me may be in them, and I in them."

Chapter 18

1 When Jesus had spoken these words, He went forth with His disciples over the ravine of the Kidron, where there was a garden, in which He entered with His disciples.

2 Now Judas also, who was betraying Him, knew the place, for Jesus had often met there with His disciples.

3 Judas then, having received the *Roman* cohort and officers from the chief priests and the Pharisees, came there with lanterns and torches and weapons.

4 So Jesus, knowing all the things that were coming upon Him, went forth and said to them, "Whom do you seek?"

5 They answered Him, "Jesus the Nazarene." He said to them, "I am *He*." And Judas also, who was betraying Him, was standing with them.

6 So when He said to them, "I am *He*," they drew back and fell to the ground.

7 Therefore He again asked them, "Whom do you seek?" And they said, "Jesus the Nazarene."

8 Jesus answered, "I told you that I am *He*; so if you seek Me, let these go their way,"

9 to fulfill the word which He spoke, "Of those whom You have given Me I lost not one."

10 Simon Peter then, having a sword, drew it and struck the high priest's slave, and cut off his right ear; and the slave's name was Malchus.

11 So Jesus said to Peter, "Put the sword into the sheath; the cup which the Father has given Me, shall I not drink it?"

12 So the *Roman* cohort and the commander and the officers of the Jews, arrested Jesus and bound Him,

13 and led Him to Annas first; for he was father-in-law of Caiaphas, who was high priest that year.

14 Now Caiaphas was the one who had advised the Jews that it was expedient for one man to die on behalf of the people.

15 Simon Peter was following Jesus, and *so was* another disciple. Now that disciple was known to the high priest, and entered with Jesus into the court of the high priest,

16 but Peter was standing at the door outside. So the other disciple, who was known to the high priest, went out and spoke to the doorkeeper, and brought Peter in.

17 Then the slave-girl who kept the door said to Peter, "You are not also *one* of this man's disciples, are you?" He said, "I am not."

18 Now the slaves and the officers were standing *there*, having made a charcoal fire, for it was cold and they were warming themselves; and Peter was also with them, standing and warming himself.

19 The high priest then questioned Jesus about His disciples, and about His teaching.

20 Jesus answered him, "I have spoken openly to the world; I always taught in synagogues and in the temple, where all the Jews come together; and I spoke nothing in secret.

21 "Why do you question Me? Question those who have heard what I spoke to them; they know what I said."

22 When He had said this, one of the officers standing nearby struck Jesus, saying, "Is that the way You answer the high priest?"

23 Jesus answered him, "If I have spoken wrongly, testify of the wrong; but if rightly, why do you strike Me?"

24 So Annas sent Him bound to Caiaphas the high priest.

25 Now Simon Peter was standing and warming himself. So they said to him, "You are not also *one* of His disciples, are you?" He denied *it*, and said, "I am not."

26 One of the slaves of the high priest, being a relative of the one whose ear Peter cut off, said, "Did I not see you in the garden with Him?"

27 Peter then denied *it* again, and immediately a rooster crowed.

28 Then they led Jesus from Caiaphas into the Praetorium, and it was early; and they themselves did not enter into the Praetorium so that they would not be defiled, but might eat the Passover.

29 Therefore Pilate went out to them and said, "What accusation do you bring against this Man?"

30 They answered and said to him, "If this Man were not an evildoer, we would not have delivered Him to you."

31 So Pilate said to them, "Take Him yourselves, and judge Him according to your law." The Jews said to him, "We are not permitted to put anyone to death,"

32 to fulfill the word of Jesus which He spoke, signifying by what kind of death He was about to die.

33 Therefore Pilate entered again into the Praetorium, and summoned Jesus and said to Him, "Are You the King of the Jews?"

34 Jesus answered, "Are you saying this on your own initiative, or did others tell you about Me?"

35 Pilate answered, "I am not a Jew, am I? Your own nation and the chief priests delivered You to me; what have You done?"

36 Jesus answered, "My kingdom is not of this world. If My kingdom were of this world, then My servants would be fighting so that I would not be handed over to the Jews; but as it is, My kingdom is not of this realm."

37 Therefore Pilate said to Him, "So You are a king?" Jesus answered, "You say *correctly* that I am a king. For this I have been born, and for this I have come into the world, to testify to the truth. Everyone who is of the truth hears My voice."
38 Pilate said to Him, "What is truth?"
And when he had said this, he went out again to the Jews and said to them, "I find no guilt in Him.
39 "But you have a custom that I release someone for you at the Passover; do you wish then that I release for you the King of the Jews?"
40 So they cried out again, saying, "Not this Man, but Barabbas." Now Barabbas was a robber.

Chapter 19
1 Pilate then took Jesus and scourged Him.
2 And the soldiers twisted together a crown of thorns and put it on His head, and put a purple robe on Him;
3 and they *began* to come up to Him and say, "Hail, King of the Jews!" and to give Him slaps *in the face*.
4 Pilate came out again and said to them, "Behold, I am bringing Him out to you so that you may know that I find no guilt in Him."
5 Jesus then came out, wearing the crown of thorns and the purple robe. *Pilate* said to them, "Behold, the Man!"
6 So when the chief priests and the officers saw Him, they cried out saying, "Crucify, crucify!" Pilate said to them, "Take Him yourselves and crucify Him, for I find no guilt in Him."
7 The Jews answered him, "We have a law, and by that law He ought to die because He made Himself out *to be* the Son of God."
8 Therefore when Pilate heard this statement, he was *even* more afraid;
9 and he entered into the Praetorium again and said to Jesus, "Where are You from?" But Jesus gave him no answer.

10 So Pilate said to Him, "You do not speak to me? Do You not know that I have authority to release You, and I have authority to crucify You?"

11 Jesus answered, "You would have no authority over Me, unless it had been given you from above; for this reason he who delivered Me to you has *the* greater sin."

12 As a result of this Pilate made efforts to release Him, but the Jews cried out saying, "If you release this Man, you are no friend of Caesar; everyone who makes himself out *to be* a king opposes Caesar."

13 Therefore when Pilate heard these words, he brought Jesus out, and sat down on the judgment seat at a place called The Pavement, but in Hebrew, Gabbatha.

14 Now it was the day of preparation for the Passover; it was about the sixth hour. And he said to the Jews, "Behold, your King!"

15 So they cried out, "Away with *Him*, away with *Him*, crucify Him!" Pilate said to them, "Shall I crucify your King?" The chief priests answered, "We have no king but Caesar."

16 So he then handed Him over to them to be crucified.

17 They took Jesus, therefore, and He went out, bearing His own cross, to the place called the Place of a Skull, which is called in Hebrew, Golgotha.

18 There they crucified Him, and with Him two other men, one on either side, and Jesus in between.

19 Pilate also wrote an inscription and put it on the cross. It was written, "JESUS THE NAZARENE, THE KING OF THE JEWS."

20 Therefore many of the Jews read this inscription, for the place where Jesus was crucified was near the city; and it was written in Hebrew, Latin *and* in Greek.

21 So the chief priests of the Jews were saying to Pilate, "Do not write, 'The King of the Jews'; but that He said, 'I am King of the Jews.'"

22 Pilate answered, "What I have written I have written."

23 Then the soldiers, when they had crucified Jesus, took His outer garments and made four parts, a part to every soldier and *also* the tunic; now the tunic was seamless, woven in one piece.

24 So they said to one another, "Let us not tear it, but cast lots for it, *to decide* whose it shall be"; *this was* to fulfill the Scripture: "THEY DIVIDED MY OUTER GARMENTS AMONG THEM, AND FOR MY CLOTHING THEY CAST LOTS."

25 Therefore the soldiers did these things.

But standing by the cross of Jesus were His mother, and His mother's sister, Mary the *wife* of Clopas, and Mary Magdalene.

26 When Jesus then saw His mother, and the disciple whom He loved standing nearby, He said to His mother, "Woman, behold, your son!"

27 Then He said to the disciple, "Behold, your mother!" From that hour the disciple took her into his own *household*.

28 After this, Jesus, knowing that all things had already been accomplished, to fulfill the Scripture, said, "I am thirsty."

29 A jar full of sour wine was standing there; so they put a sponge full of the sour wine upon *a branch of* hyssop and brought it up to His mouth.

30 Therefore when Jesus had received the sour wine, He said, "It is finished!" And He bowed His head and gave up His spirit.

31 Then the Jews, because it was the day of preparation, so that the bodies would not remain on the cross on the Sabbath (for that Sabbath was a high day), asked Pilate that their legs might be broken, and *that* they might be taken away.

32 So the soldiers came, and broke the legs of the first man and of the other who was crucified with Him;

33 but coming to Jesus, when they saw that He was already dead, they did not break His legs.

34 But one of the soldiers pierced His side with a spear, and immediately blood and water came out.

35 And he who has seen has testified, and his testimony is true; and he knows that he is telling the truth, so that you also may believe.

36 For these things came to pass to fulfill the Scripture, "NOT A BONE OF HIM SHALL BE BROKEN."

37 And again another Scripture says, "THEY SHALL LOOK ON HIM WHOM THEY PIERCED."

38 After these things Joseph of Arimathea, being a disciple of Jesus, but a secret *one* for fear of the Jews, asked Pilate that he might take away the body of Jesus; and Pilate granted permission. So he came and took away His body.

39 Nicodemus, who had first come to Him by night, also came, bringing a mixture of myrrh and aloes, about a hundred pounds *weight*.

40 So they took the body of Jesus and bound it in linen wrappings with the spices, as is the burial custom of the Jews.

41 Now in the place where He was crucified there was a garden, and in the garden a new tomb in which no one had yet been laid.

42 Therefore because of the Jewish day of preparation, since the tomb was nearby, they laid Jesus there.

Chapter 20

1 Now on the first *day* of the week Mary Magdalene came early to the tomb, while it was still dark, and saw the stone *already* taken away from the tomb.

2 So she ran and came to Simon Peter and to the other disciple whom Jesus loved, and said to them, "They have taken away the

Lord out of the tomb, and we do not know where they have laid Him."

3 So Peter and the other disciple went forth, and they were going to the tomb.

4 The two were running together; and the other disciple ran ahead faster than Peter and came to the tomb first;

5 and stooping and looking in, he saw the linen wrappings lying *there*; but he did not go in.

6 And so Simon Peter also came, following him, and entered the tomb; and he saw the linen wrappings lying *there*,

7 and the face-cloth which had been on His head, not lying with the linen wrappings, but rolled up in a place by itself.

8 So the other disciple who had first come to the tomb then also entered, and he saw and believed.

9 For as yet they did not understand the Scripture, that He must rise again from the dead.

10 So the disciples went away again to their own homes.

11 But Mary was standing outside the tomb weeping; and so, as she wept, she stooped and looked into the tomb;

12 and she saw two angels in white sitting, one at the head and one at the feet, where the body of Jesus had been lying.

13 And they said to her, "Woman, why are you weeping?" She said to them, "Because they have taken away my Lord, and I do not know where they have laid Him."

14 When she had said this, she turned around and saw Jesus standing *there*, and did not know that it was Jesus.

15 Jesus said to her, "Woman, why are you weeping? Whom are you seeking?" Supposing Him to be the gardener, she said to Him, "Sir, if you have carried Him away, tell me where you have laid Him, and I will take Him away."

16 Jesus said to her, "Mary!" She turned and said to Him in Hebrew, "Rabboni!" (which means, Teacher).

17 Jesus said to her, "Stop clinging to Me, for I have not yet ascended to the Father; but go to My brethren and say to them, 'I ascend to My Father and your Father, and My God and your God.'"

18 Mary Magdalene came, announcing to the disciples, "I have seen the Lord," and *that* He had said these things to her.

19 So when it was evening on that day, the first *day* of the week, and when the doors were shut where the disciples were, for fear of the Jews, Jesus came and stood in their midst and said to them, "Peace *be* with you."

20 And when He had said this, He showed them both His hands and His side. The disciples then rejoiced when they saw the Lord.

21 So Jesus said to them again, "Peace *be* with you; as the Father has sent Me, I also send you."

22 And when He had said this, He breathed on them and said to them, "Receive the Holy Spirit.

23 "If you forgive the sins of any, *their sins* have been forgiven them; if you retain the *sins* of any, they have been retained."

24 But Thomas, one of the twelve, called Didymus, was not with them when Jesus came.

25 So the other disciples were saying to him, "We have seen the Lord!" But he said to them, "Unless I see in His hands the imprint of the nails, and put my finger into the place of the nails, and put my hand into His side, I will not believe."

26 After eight days His disciples were again inside, and Thomas with them. Jesus came, the doors having been shut, and stood in their midst and said, "Peace *be* with you."

27 Then He said to Thomas, "Reach here with your finger, and see My hands; and reach here your hand and put it into My side; and do not be unbelieving, but believing."

28 Thomas answered and said to Him, "My Lord and my God!"

29 Jesus said to him, "Because you have seen Me, have you believed? Blessed *are* they who did not see, and *yet* believed."

30 Therefore many other signs Jesus also performed in the presence of the disciples, which are not written in this book;

31 but these have been written so that you may believe that Jesus is the Christ, the Son of God; and that believing you may have life in His name.

Chapter 21

1 After these things Jesus manifested Himself again to the disciples at the Sea of Tiberias, and He manifested *Himself* in this way.

2 Simon Peter, and Thomas called Didymus, and Nathanael of Cana in Galilee, and the *sons* of Zebedee, and two others of His disciples were together.

3 Simon Peter said to them, "I am going fishing." They said to him, "We will also come with you." They went out and got into the boat; and that night they caught nothing.

4 But when the day was now breaking, Jesus stood on the beach; yet the disciples did not know that it was Jesus.

5 So Jesus said to them, "Children, you do not have any fish, do you?" They answered Him, "No."

6 And He said to them, "Cast the net on the right-hand side of the boat and you will find *a catch*." So they cast, and then they were not able to haul it in because of the great number of fish.

7 Therefore that disciple whom Jesus loved said to Peter, "It is the Lord." So when Simon Peter heard that it was the Lord, he put his outer garment on (for he was stripped *for work*), and threw himself into the sea.

8 But the other disciples came in the little boat, for they were not far from the land, but about one hundred yards away, dragging the net *full* of fish.

9 So when they got out on the land, they saw a charcoal fire *already* laid and fish placed on it, and bread.

10 Jesus said to them, "Bring some of the fish which you have now caught."

11 Simon Peter went up and drew the net to land, full of large fish, a hundred and fifty-three; and although there were so many, the net was not torn.

12 Jesus said to them, "Come *and* have breakfast." None of the disciples ventured to question Him, "Who are You?" knowing that it was the Lord.

13 Jesus came and took the bread and gave *it* to them, and the fish likewise.

14 This is now the third time that Jesus was manifested to the disciples, after He was raised from the dead.

15 So when they had finished breakfast, Jesus said to Simon Peter, "Simon, *son* of John, do you love Me more than these?" He said to Him, "Yes, Lord; You know that I love You." He said to him, "Tend My lambs."

16 He said to him again a second time, "Simon, *son* of John, do you love Me?" He said to Him, "Yes, Lord; You know that I love You." He said to him, "Shepherd My sheep."

17 He said to him the third time, "Simon, *son* of John, do you love Me?" Peter was grieved because He said to him the third time, "Do you love Me?" And he said to Him, "Lord, You know all things; You know that I love You." Jesus said to him, "Tend My sheep.

18 "Truly, truly, I say to you, when you were younger, you used to gird yourself and walk wherever you wished; but when you grow old, you will stretch out your hands and someone else will gird you, and bring you where you do not wish to *go*."

19 Now this He said, signifying by what kind of death he would glorify God. And when He had spoken this, He said to him, "Follow Me!"

20 Peter, turning around, saw the disciple whom Jesus loved following *them*; the one who also had leaned back on His bosom at the supper and said, "Lord, who is the one who betrays You?"

21 So Peter seeing him said to Jesus, "Lord, and what about this man?"

22 Jesus said to him, "If I want him to remain until I come, what *is that* to you? You follow Me!"

23 Therefore this saying went out among the brethren that that disciple would not die; yet Jesus did not say to him that he would not die, but *only*, "If I want him to remain until I come, what *is that* to you?"

24 This is the disciple who is testifying to these things and wrote these things, and we know that his testimony is true.

25 And there are also many other things which Jesus did, which if they were written in detail, I suppose that even the world itself would not contain the books that would be written.

JOHN AT A GLANCE

eme of John:

SEGMENT DIVISIONS

PORTRAYALS OF JESUS CHRIST	SIGNS AND MIRACLES	MINISTRY	CHAPTER THEMES
		TO ISRAEL	1
			2
			3
			4
			5
			6
			7
			8
			9
			10
			11
		TO DISCIPLES	12
			13
			14
			15
			16
			17
		TO ALL MANKIND	18
			19
			20
		TO DISCIPLES	21

Author:

Date:

Purpose:

Key Words:
(including synonyms)

THE FEASTS OF ISRAEL

	1st Month (Nisan) Festival of Passover *(Pesach)*				3rd Month (Sivan) Festival of Pentecost *(Shav*
Slaves in Egypt	**Passover**	**Unleavened Bread**	**First fruits**		**Pentecost or Feast of Weeks**
	Kill lamb & put blood on doorpost Exodus 12:6,7	*Purging of all leaven* (symbol of sin)	*Wave offering of sheaf* (promise of harvest to come)		*Wave offering of two loaves of leavened bread*
	1st month, 14th day Leviticus 23:5	1st month, 15th day for 7 days Leviticus 23:6-8 *(1st and 7th days are Sabbath)*	Day after Sabbath Leviticus 23:9-14 *(It is a Sabbath)*		50 days after first fruits Leviticus 23:15-21 *(It is a Sabbath)*
Whosoever commits sin is the slave to sin	**Christ our Passover has been sacrificed**	**Clean out old leaven... just as you are in fact unleavened**	**Christ has been raised...the first fruits**	**Going away so Comforter can come**	**Promise of the Spirit mystery of church: Jews-Gentiles in one body**
				Mount of Olives	
John 8:34	1 Corinthians 5:7	1 Corinthians 5:7,8	1 Corinthians 15:20-23	John 16:7 Acts 1:9-12	Acts 2:1-47 1 Corinthians 12:13 Ephesians 2:11-22

	7th Month (Tishri) Festival of Tabernacles *(Succoth)*		
	Feast of Trumpets	**Day of Atonement**	**Feast of Booths or Tabernacles**
Interlude Between Festivals	*Trumpet blown — a holy convocation*	*Atonement shall be made to cleanse you* Leviticus 16:30	*Harvest celebration memorial of tabernacles in wilderness*
	7th month, 1st day Leviticus 23:23-25 *(It is a Sabbath)*	7th month, 10th day Leviticus 23:26-32 *(It is a Sabbath)*	7th month, 15th day, for 7 days; 8th day, Holy Convocation Leviticus 23:33-44 *(The 1st and 8th days are Sabbaths)*
	Regathering of Israel in preparation for final day of atonement Jeremiah 32:37-41	**Israel will repent and look to Messiah in one day** Zechariah 3:9,10; 12:10; 13:1; 14:9 Coming of Christ	**Families of the earth will come to Jerusalem to celebrate the Feast of Booths** Zechariah 14:16-19
	Ezekiel 36:24	Ezekiel 36:25-27 Hebrews 9,10 Romans 11:25-29	Ezekiel 36:28

New heaven and new earth

God tabernacles with men
Revelation 21:1-3

Israel had two harvests each year—spring and autumn

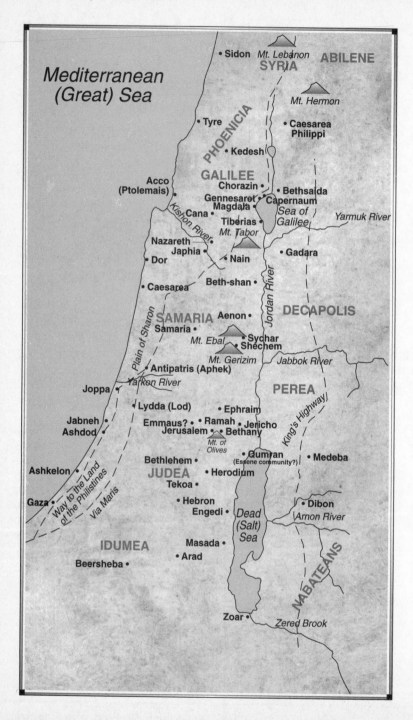

Leader's Guide

The Two Ways to Do This Study

The first way you can do this study with others is do the assignments together with the class. You go through the book doing one assignment at a time and then discussing what the student or students learned. The pace you keep depends on the amount of time you have; therefore you ignore "weeks" and "days" and do whatever you can. The one caution is not to drag it out so long that you lose your students.

If someone is new to Bible study or is not a believer in Jesus Christ, this is a life-changing way to mentor them and encourage them along the way. You could have no higher calling than to introduce another person to the very words of God so they can know you can "discover truth for yourself."

Because we live in a time when people are so busy and overworked that they don't feel they have time to study on their own, this way of conducting the study enables you to meet them where they are and introduce them to the immeasurable benefit of studying God's Word for their spiritual health and well-being.

If you do the study this way, it will be important for you as the leader to do the week's study in advance so you are prepared to direct the students and help them in their quest for truth. You will find discussion questions in the next segment, which are simply there to help you should you need it.

(By the way, this book has been used to teach English to many precious people all around the world.)

The second way you can use this book is to have the students do the assignments on their own and then come together for discussion. If you do this, it is still good to do the first two lessons (or portions of the lessons) together with them to make sure they understand what they are doing.

Preparing to Lead the Class

Each week you will be given suggestions as to how you may want to review the material your class members studied individually that week. For instance, after they complete the lesson for Week 1, the group would then meet to discuss the material.* Please know the proposed leader questions are suggestions only!

As you prepare for each class session you should come before the Father in prayer and ask Him to help you. You can trust that He will show you what to add to the suggestions or what to subtract from them. He may even redirect you as you wait before Him for His leading. He alone knows the need of each group member, and in His faithfulness He will show you how to take what has been studied and move through it so that He can apply it in the most effective way. Trust Him, dear leader.

Know, too, that this book has been translated into a host of languages and used in groups with people from a variety of backgrounds representing numerous cultures. You will need to seek the Father in light of the background and culture of the group in which you are using the materials.

During the first lessons of this study, you may want to take the homework questions one by one and see how the students answered them and whether or not they have any questions. Remember to encourage, encourage, encourage! And if their answers are wrong, show them how to find the right answers.

---

* Teaching CDs that can be used after the discussion time to reinforce and enhance the study are available from Precept Ministries, P.O. Box 182218, Chattanooga, TN 37422. These tapes are in English.

Begin Each Session with Prayer

I would urge you to begin each session with prayer and ask the Holy Spirit to meet with you and to use what is shared to encourage, challenge, and refine everyone's lives. Ask Him, in the presence of the group, to create an atmosphere of loving acceptance, where each person is free to share what he or she has learned.

Create a Relaxed Atmosphere Where All Can Share

As you lead and as people share, be sure that you don't embarrass anyone who doesn't give what you consider a "right answer." Create a relaxed atmosphere. Tell them that all of you are learning and that sometimes we learn best when we give a wrong answer. We then learn the correct answer and won't forget it!

If you are hard on the group members, you will discourage discussion. But if you encourage and create an atmosphere in which people know that you accept them as they are, they will be eager to discuss what they are seeing and learning. You'll create an air of excitement.

Know, too, that some people in the class may have other questions that you do not plan to cover. If you do not have time to deal with the questions or you feel they don't understand enough of God's Word for you to provide an answer, make note of their questions. Tell them that you want to wait to answer these questions until the class sees what God's Word says as they continue their study.

Helpful Tools for Your Time Together

It is helpful if you can obtain a white marker board so that you can record some of the insights that are shared. It is helpful to have a record of what is shared in front of the class so they can *see* as well as hear what is being learned. Seeing the insights listed on a board will help cement God's truth in the minds and hearts of the group.

For Your First Meeting Together

Typically, your discussion time with the students will follow a week of study in which they have seen God's truth for themselves. However, during your *first* meeting you should go through the introductory material. Please read "Discussion of the Material That Precedes Week 1" and know that you are beginning an awesome adventure, for you will see God work in wondrous ways!

You Are Prayed For and Appreciated

Know that I have prayed for you, and you can trust our God to work in and through you as you make yourself available to Him!

Discussion of the Material that Precedes Week 1

Since the class has not yet begun their weekly studies, use the first meeting to walk through the material with the group.

Begin by telling the class that your study will be a process where truth is built upon truth. Let them know that as they study God's Word with diligence, they will discover what He wants to teach them individually *and* that they will be enriched by hearing others share what He has shown them.

Begin with prayer, Beloved. This is God's book, and you will want to acknowledge your dependence upon Him. Ask the Holy Spirit to meet with you as a class each week as you spend time in His Word. Pray that each person will see how the truth of God's Word applies to him or her personally.

Have the group read the section that leads up to Week 1. If there are people in your class who are slow readers or slow learners, encourage them to stay with the study even though they may struggle. Let them know that when they complete this course, they will have developed study skills that can help them excel in other kinds of study.

Suggest to the class members that they underline or highlight important points as they read. Underlining makes it easier to go back and review key facts or truths. For instance, under the heading WHAT IS THE BIBLE? they might want to highlight or underline "The Bible...is a book made up of 66 separate books" and "the first part is called the Old Testament and the second part is called the New Testament." Encourage the students to underline the most important facts.

After the class finishes reading, discuss what they learned about the Bible and why it is important to study it. During this discussion, be sure to stress the importance of knowing about the God of the Bible and what the Bible says. *At this point, really encourage your students! Your excitement and passion to know truth by knowing God's Word will be contagious. Share what God can and will do for them if they will persevere to the end of the study. Remember, the words of God are spirit and life. Explain that when they study the Bible, they are studying a book like no other book in the world. It is a book that changes lives as well as the course of history.*

Next, discuss the purpose of the Gospel of John. Have someone read John 20:30-31 and, if a board is available, write the passage so everyone in the class can see it. Then under John 20:30-31, list the main points of these verses.

Ask the questions listed below and put the answers on the board. (At this point I will supply you with the answers for these questions so we can be sure to begin on track together. I will not provide answers, however, in the remainder of the leader section.) Instruct your students to go to the Bible text for their answers. This will show them that the Bible gives us the answers we need and that we don't have to come up with answers of our own. The Bible tells us everything we need to know; we simply need to carefully observe (see) what it says.

1. Why was the Gospel of John written?

    a. so that you may believe that Jesus is the Christ, the Son of God

Discuss with your group that the word *Christ* is another way of saying "Messiah." The Messiah was the One who God promised to send to His people to save them from their sins and to eventually rule as King over all the earth. He would be God's one and only Son and would be just like the Father. Therefore, to say that Jesus is the Son of God is to say that Jesus *is* God. Your students should watch for any verses which show that Jesus is God and that Jesus is the same as God the Father in His character and His power.

    b. that believing you may have life in His [Jesus'] name

Those who confess the Lord Jesus Christ as their Savior and Lord have life in Jesus' name. In other words, when they truly believe in Jesus, He gives them His life. As your group continues this study, tell them to watch carefully what the Gospel of John says about those who truly believe.

You will want to mention that in biblical times, names were very important. They often described the person—what he was, or what he was called to do. To speak or to act in another person's name would be to speak and act according to what that person's name meant or the authority it carried. For instance, when a police officer pounds on someone's door, he will say, "Open up in the name of the law." The police officer is standing there as a representative of the law.

2. What does the Gospel of John record so that people may believe that Jesus is the Son of God, the Christ?

    a. signs that Jesus performed in the presence of His disciples

3. Why did John tell us that Jesus' signs were performed in the presence of His disciples? Does it make any difference that they saw these signs? What difference would it make? (As your group thinks about this, try to apply it to them. For example, if you are talking to people who have been tried by our courts of justice, ask them how important eyewitnesses are and why.)

4. Now that you know John's purpose for writing, what should you watch for as you read and study the Gospel of John?

    a. things which show that Jesus is the Christ, the Son of God

    b. various signs Jesus did, WHERE He did them, WHAT they were, WHAT happened, and WHO saw them

    c. HOW the various people who saw these signs reacted to them and WHY

5. When you finish this discussion, you may want to start your students on Week 1's homework. Helping them begin the homework will make it easier and will be an encouragement to them.

If you have the class begin the homework, plan to review with them Day One and Day Two. Ask them to work through Day One and discuss what they saw. Then do Day Two. After they read and mark every reference to *the Word* as well as the pronouns and synonyms, read John1:1-18 aloud. Tell them to shout "Word" each time you come to a reference to the *Word* they marked (or colored). This way, they can see what they should have marked.

6. When you finish, suggest that the group talk to God in prayer. Tell them to share with God what is on their hearts, what they need, what they want to learn, and why. Try to have conversational prayer in which everyone in the group is free to be silent or to pray without feeling uncomfortable.

Tell your class you will do the study up to Week 7, and if any of them want to finish the last six weeks, you'll continue. Ask each person to commit to being faithful to study for at least seven weeks and to hold one another accountable.

Encourage your class to complete next week's lesson, Week 1 (unless, of course, you do the work together). Tell them to do as much as they can and not to worry if they don't understand it all or can't get it all done. Tell them not to be afraid of wrong answers because you all are learning together. Share with them that they will meet obstacles. (Satan doesn't want them to know God's Word, as it is the Christian's means of defeating him.) Encourage them to press on no matter what—the reward they will receive is invaluable!

Beloved, pray for your class. Prayer and the Word are the two things which make the greatest difference in people's lives. As a leader, you have the opportunity to deposit both in their lives!

Week 1

1. Begin in prayer, asking God to be with each member of the class and help him or her understand what His Word says.

2. Read John chapter 1 aloud. Tell the class that as you read, you want them to shout "Word, or Jesus" every time you come to a word they marked that refers to *the Word* (the Word is identified as Jesus in verse 17) and to shout "John" every time you mention a reference to John the Baptist. This process will help the students be certain they marked the right words along with each word's synonyms and pronouns.

3. Have the class tell you everything they learned about Jesus from John 1. Ask them which verse or verses gave them the information. Record on the board each insight that is shared.

4. When you finish, write John 20:30-31 on the board. Ask the students what they saw in John 1 that was written in order to help John fulfill his purpose for writing his Gospel. List on the board what is shared, and put a checkmark next to each item that shows that Jesus is the Christ or the Son of God.

5. Ask your students if any signs are recorded in John 1. (Although the answer is no, have them see where in chapter 1 John lets his readers know that Jesus is the Christ, the Son of God, and that He is beginning to accomplish His purpose.)

6. Ask the group what they learned about John the Baptist. Talk about his relationship to Jesus Christ. Then ask what they learned about John that they can apply to their own lives.

Discuss John's attitude toward Jesus and what he tells others about Jesus. Suggest to your students that they pray and ask God for opportunities to share the truths they are learning about Jesus. Tell them that God will show them who to talk with by putting the thought in their mind and causing them to want to share with that person.

However, if the group members live among people who do not like Christians, before they speak about Jesus, they should let others see the difference that Jesus makes in the way they live. Then they should pray that people will ask them why they are different. Tell your students to pray much before they speak and to always share what God's Word says. When they quote or read the Bible to others, they must remember that God's Word is filled with life. It's a supernatural book, and God will use it in a supernatural way.

7. You may also want to go over the questions that were asked in the lesson and see how the students answered them. Be sure to discuss what they learned about sin.

8. A good exercise for your students is to have them go to five different people, individually or in small groups, and ask the people they approach whether they would mind helping them complete an assignment for the course they're taking. Have your students ask God to direct them in who they are to approach, and encourage them to be pleasant and engaging. Here are the specific steps:

Course Assignment

1. Ask the people you approach if they could give you ten to fifteen minutes of their time and critique you on the way you present the lesson.

2. Hand each individual a copy of John 1:1-18 along with a pencil or pen and ask them if they would read this section with you and circle every reference to "the Word" as you read the Scripture verses to them.

3. Read the first three verses and then ask them what they learn about "the Word" from marking it with a circle. If they ask who "the Word" is, tell them they need to wait and see whether the text tells them. Ask them to watch for the answer.

4. When you are finished, move to the next few scriptures and read, mark, and discuss what they learn.

5. When you complete the text, ask them what they thought about what they learned from the Word of God. At this point you need to be praying fervently for the leadership of God's Spirit in the conversation.

6. At the end, hand the person you've been talking with the form on the opposite page (you may photocopy it if you like) and ask them to fill it out.

Week 2

This week you will cover John 2 and 3 with your class. Because John 3 is such a wonderful chapter, make sure you don't take up too much time discussing John 2. As you lead your discussion, ask God to speak in a powerful way to the students so that they might understand 1) what it means to believe in Jesus Christ, and 2) what happens if they don't believe.

Response Sheet

Thank you for taking the time to critique this student on his or her lesson presentation. Your responses will be evaluated by the student's instructor, and if you write them on this sheet, the student will receive a higher grade.

1. Please list the points about "the Word" that you learned from the text.

2. Briefly, what is the relationship between "the Word" and the people in the text?

3. What can "the Word" do for people?

As you pray, ask God to cause your students to be born again through this study if they haven't already become true Christians. Don't try to push them to believe; let God and His Spirit do their work through His Word. If your students are already saved, pray that they might become mighty men and women of God who will love Him and proclaim His Word.

1. Discuss the first sign Jesus did. Tell the class you are going to ask the 5 W's and an H about this sign. Ask the group to state what verse in John 2 contains the answer they share. You might ask them the following:

   a. WHAT was the first sign Jesus did?

   b. WHERE was the sign performed?

   c. WHO saw the sign?

   d. WHY was the sign performed?

   e. WHAT happened as a result of this sign?

2. Ask the group where else the word *sign* or *signs* is mentioned in John 2. Ask what they learned from marking the word in that verse. Once again, ask the 5 W's and an H. Remember, you don't always find all the answers to the 5 W's and an H; you only find out what the text tells you.

Don't miss the "sign" of the resurrection of Jesus Christ from the dead, which is mentioned in John 2:18-22. Also, notice what the disciples remember after Jesus' resurrection (Jesus being raised from the dead). We will study more about the resurrection in John 20.

3. Ask where the word *believe* and its synonyms are used in John 2. As your class gives each reference, ask what they learned from marking the word. Ask WHO believed, WHY they believed, and WHAT they believed.

4. Now move on to John chapter 3 by discussing what happened to Nicodemus when he talked with Jesus. Once again, ask the 5 W's and an H. WHO was Nicodemus? WHEN did Nicodemus go to Jesus? WHY did he go to see Jesus? HOW did Nicodemus address Jesus—what did he call Him? WHAT did Jesus tell Nicodemus? WHAT does *born again* mean? HOW does it happen? Can you see it happen, or can you see only the results? What is it like? (Discuss the fact that you cannot see the wind itself, but only the effects of the wind.)

5. Ask the class to tell you what they learned from marking the word *believe* in John 3. List their insights on the board. You might want to make two columns: **Those Who Believe** and **Those Who Do Not Believe**.

6. Ask the class what they learned about God from this chapter and list their answers on the board. Then ask them how this compares with what they previously thought about God. If there are any students who believe in other gods or prophets, you might want to list on the board what they believe about their god or prophet. Then they can compare God Almighty with their god.

7. Discuss the themes of John 1, 2, and 3. Have the class share their themes for these chapters. Let them see that once they discover the main point, subject, or events of each chapter, the theme can be said or expressed in different ways. Although each person will state the theme in his or her own way, it is important that everyone sees what the chapter deals with the most. For example:

a. John 1 tells about the Word who was made flesh (John 1:14) and John the Baptist's testimony about Jesus.

b. John 2 deals with the first sign, turning water into wine. That is the main point. But students can also mention the sign of the temple of Jesus' body being raised (which would happen later).

c. John 3 deals with being born again. It also talks about John the Baptist's testimony.

8. Conclude the session with prayer and encourage the class to work through Week 3 in preparation for your next meeting.

Week 3

1. Begin your class by writing the titles for three columns on the board: **The Samaritans' Worship, The Jews' Worship, True Worship**. Using the 5 W's and an H, ask the class what they learned about the Samaritans' worship. For example, WHERE do Samaritans worship? WHAT do they worship? HOW? and so on. Then fill in the second column (**The Jews' Worship**) in the same way. Be sure to discuss what John 4 teaches about true worship of the Father. Record the group's insights on the board under the appropriate column title.

2. Even though the Samaritan woman worshiped differently from Jesus, lived an immoral lifestyle, and was of a different class or race from Jesus, what was Jesus' attitude toward her?

Discuss how Jesus dealt with the woman. Point out that He did not ignore her sinful lifestyle, but instead, exposed it. Notice He did not put her down; He simply let her see her sin so she could desire the water of life that He was offering to her.

Next, talk about Jesus' attitude toward the woman and compare that with the disciples' apparent attitude. Does this show the difference that Christianity should make in the treatment of a woman? Ask your class what they learned about women from the way Jesus treated the Samaritan woman. (Remember, Jesus *had* to go through Samaria. Ask the students why. Be sure they see that there was a woman who needed Jesus—a woman who would tell others about

Him when she discovered who He was. May the women in your class do the same!)

Special note: Depending on the culture in which you are presenting this material, you may want to point out that in many places women are not properly esteemed. Baby girls are sometimes put to death simply because they are girls. But, according to Psalm 139:13, "You [God] formed my inward parts; You wove me in my mother's womb. I will give thanks to You, for I am fearfully and wonderfully made; wonderful are Your works, and my soul knows it very well." Therefore, when someone puts a baby to death, he is killing what God created. God will have to judge that person, for he committed murder. The Bible says, "Whoever sheds man's blood, by man his blood shall be shed, for in the image of God He made man" (Genesis 9:6).

In many cultures, men are allowed to beat their wives, put them down, and divorce them at any time for any reason. You may want to read Ephesians 5:18-33 and note how men who are filled with God's Spirit will treat their wives and how wives are to respond to their husbands.

3. Discuss what the class learned from marking the word *believe*. Ask how believing what they have studied these past three weeks would affect their relationship with God, with Jesus, and with others.

4. Talk about the second sign Jesus performed, using the 5 W's and an H. Make sure you discuss what this sign shows about Jesus. Have the students turn to their JOHN AT A GLANCE chart (page 217). Under the column marked "Signs," record the first two signs in the book of John next to the chapter in which each is recorded. Then tell the class to remind you every time they need to record another sign in this column.

5. Ask the class to share what they learned from chapter 5 about the Son and the Father. List on the board what the class shares about **God the Father** in one column and **God the Son** in another column. Then discuss how Jesus' life and behavior showed what the Father is like. Stop and think of the ways that Jesus lived and related to people in the first three chapters of John.

6. Finally, ask your students how their worship compares with a true worship of God. Ask how they should relate to the Father and Son in light of what they learned from seeing Jesus' relationship to the Father.

7. Discuss the themes of John 4 and 5. Have the class share their themes from their JOHN AT A GLANCE chart (page 217).

8. If there is time, give the class an opportunity to share what is happening in their lives as a result of doing this study. If anyone is having a hard time, ask everyone to pray for that person. Remember that the members of the class should show a genuine concern for one another. You as a leader can model this for them by your love, concern, and prayers.

Week 4

1. List on the board the signs mentioned or done in John 6. Be sure to record the signs not specifically mentioned but referred to in John 6:2. Record the sign of multiplying the loaves and fishes, and use the 5 W's and an H to discuss this sign. Be sure to talk about the people's response to this sign and why the crowds started to follow Jesus. Also, don't miss the sign of Jesus walking on the water. WHO saw it? WHAT did it show?

2. Make a list of all the class learned from John 6 about the true bread which comes down from heaven.

a. Read Exodus 16:1-31 and explain what manna was. WHAT did the Israelites eat each day? WHAT were they to do with it? Use this Bible passage to start a discussion about Jesus being the bread of life.

b. If there is time and you are so led by the Spirit of God, you may also want to share Deuteronomy 8:3 with your class so they can see the importance of reading and studying God's Word every day, which helps them know how they are to live.

c. Discuss what is meant by the Scriptures that say we are to eat His flesh and drink His blood. (Help the students see that this is simply another way of saying that they are to believe on Jesus, to receive Him as their Lord and Savior, to make Him a part of their lives, to invite Him to live within them, to identify with Jesus.)

d. You may want to read Matthew 26:26-29 and 1 Corinthians 11:23-26 and explain that the Lord's Supper (1 Corinthians 11:20) is an activity that the church does periodically as a remembrance that Jesus died for our sins, and that we, by believing in Him, receive Him as our Lord and Savior and are brought into a covenant agreement with Him.

A covenant is a solemn, binding agreement. John 1:17 tells us that the Law (that is, the Old Covenant or Old Testament) came by Moses and that grace and truth were realized through Jesus Christ. When Jesus Christ came, He made a new covenant, a covenant of grace.

Grace is unearned favor. Even though we were sinners, God loved us and gave us favor by offering us the free gift of eternal life— a gift we can receive by believing on Jesus Christ, who died and paid for all our sins. This is the covenant in His blood, spoken of in

Matthew 26:26-29 and 1 Corinthians 11. The New Testament is the New Covenant, the covenant of grace. The Old Testament is the Old Covenant, the Law.

3. If there is time, review what the students listed about eternal life from John 6 and how it relates to John 20:30-31. Then discuss what the chapter teaches about being raised from the dead.

4. Talk about the ways various people responded to the teaching of Jesus and what this chapter tells us about Judas. Point out that not everyone will believe what God's Word says and receive Jesus Christ as Lord and Savior. Discuss what this chapter teaches about those who do not believe, and compare that with what happens to those who do believe.

5. Note what feast was at hand. If there is time, explain the Passover from Exodus 12:1–13:16. Have the class look at the chart THE FEASTS OF ISRAEL and explain that the Jews went to Jerusalem every year to celebrate this feast.

6. Discuss the theme of John 6.

7. End the session with sharing and prayer. Ask God to show you how to create an atmosphere in which people feel the liberty to share whatever they think or believe about what they are studying. Don't argue with them; simply point out what the Word of God says, and let God do the rest. You cannot save these people or change them, only God can do that. Pray, pray, pray! Many times as people start to explain what they think, they see for themselves whether or not their reasoning is correct.

Week 5

1. Discuss the content of John 7. Move through it paragraph by paragraph, asking the 5 W's and an H in each paragraph. Have the class point out who the people are and how they respond. When the students mention the Feast of Booths, look at it on the chart THE FEASTS OF ISRAEL, noting the time of year.

2. Ask the class to look through the Observation Worksheets and share what they learned as they marked *the Christ*. List their insights on the board. Be sure everyone remembers that John's purpose was to show them that Jesus is *the Christ*, the Son of God.

3. Discuss insights about the Spirit from John 7:37-39. Note WHO the Spirit was given to, WHEN He would be given, and HOW He is described.

The Greek verbs for *come* and *drink* in John 7:37 are in the present tense. In Greek, the present tense signifies continuous or habitual action. Point out that this shows our continued dependence upon Jesus Christ. Remind your students that this is the way we saw Jesus live in relationship to the Father in John 5:19,30.

4. Ask the group to share what they learned about sin by marking the word in John 8. List on the board what is shared.

a. Have the class name some sins that people are slaves to. Tell them that when a person first commits a specific sin, he is setting himself up to commit that sin again, and again, and again, until he is a slave to that sin. The following are some examples:

1) A person may begin looking at magazines that appeal to his sexual desires. If this isn't stopped, the person will desire and want to try what he is seeing, until finally he is enslaved by the thoughts, the desires, and then the actions.

2) Someone may tell just one lie or cheat just one time. If he is not caught, he may continue to do it, and eventually lying or cheating will become a habit.

3) Someone may try a drug that is supposed to help him sleep or to deal with physical pain. It helps, so he tries it just once more. But then he ends up wanting more and more, and he can become addicted.

b. During this discussion, look at what God says about sexual sins. Have someone read Leviticus 20:10-16 on pages 67-68 and then talk about the various kinds of sexual sin mentioned. This is important, for these sins are found in every culture.

Make sure your students know that if someone commits a sexual sin against them, God will judge that person. (Ask God to make you sensitive to the needs of the class, because approximately one out of every three or four women are victims of sexual abuse, and so are many men.) Remind the group that God knows what happened and He wants to help them be healed of sin's wounds. He also wants them to forgive those who abused them so that they can press on toward His high calling on their lives. Share Romans 8:28-30 and Philippians 3:7-14, and pray for them.

c. Make sure you mention that Jesus is the only One who can set us free from slavery to sin. He tells us the truth. We believe it, receive Him, and He sets us free from our slavery.

5. Discuss the contrast between Jesus and the Jews in John 8:21-23 and the contrast between Jesus and the devil, who is described in John 8:44. List these on the board.

6. Make sure the class understands the importance of Jesus' statement, "Unless you believe that I am *He*, you will die in your sins" (John 8:24).

Every true believer will agree that Jesus is God in the flesh, one with and equal to the Father. Jesus is God. He is deity. (Mention that the word *deity* means that Jesus is God, one with the Father, equal to the Father.) The cults, however, deny the absolute deity of Jesus Christ. Instead, they say He is *a* god, or that we are gods.

Compare what the class learned about the deity of Christ in John 8 with John's purpose for writing his Gospel as stated in John 20:30-31. Also, have the class review what they have learned about Jesus from John 1–8 that shows Jesus is God in the flesh.

7. Do not forget to talk about the themes of John 7 and 8.

8. Give the class a chance to express how they feel about all they have studied so far. Ask them to share any questions they have. Ask if anyone has come to believe in Jesus and receive Him as his or her Lord and Savior since beginning this study. If so, give that person an opportunity to share about it.

9. Close in prayer. Urge those who are not yet believers to talk openly and honestly to God about it and to tell God that they really want to know the truth, for the truth sets people free.

Week 6

1. Ask the class to examine the sign recorded in John 9 by using the 5 W's and an H. Write these headings on the board: **Jesus, The Blind Man, His Parents, The Jews.** Record all that is seen about these people, their hearts, and their attitude toward Jesus and others.

As you discuss the Jews, make sure the class notices that the Jews threatened to put the blind man and his parents out of the synagogue. The synagogue was very important to Jewish families since it was the center of their worship—the place where they studied the Word of God. It was also a place of fellowship. Being put out of the synagogue would be like being cast out of a church, mosque, or temple. Such an action on the part of the Jewish religious leaders would make the blind man and his family outcasts.

It's important to note that, in some cultures, new believers are thrown out of their homes and taken away from their spouses, family, and children. Often they are persecuted. Sometimes their lives are even threatened; in some parts of the world, if a person turns from his religion to Christianity, he is put to death.

What, then, is the comfort and hope of those who are rejected by their family, friends, community, and religious leaders because of their faith in the Lord Jesus Christ? It is the truths of John 10—so let's move now into this chapter.

2. On the board write three headings: **The Shepherd, The Sheep, The Thief.** Then have the class tell you everything they learned from John 10 about these three and record their insights on the board. (At this point, do not discuss the section in the book called INSIGHTS ON SHEEP. That will come later.)

As you discuss the wonderful truths of John 10, be sensitive to your students and their insights. There are so many awesome assurances in this chapter that you don't want to rush them. Let them share. Have each person tell you which verses gave them their insights. This will keep the group true to the Word of God.

3. Discuss why Jesus told this "figure of speech" (John 10:6) to the Pharisees (John 9:40-41) and how the Pharisees reacted to it.

4. Next, have the class share what they learned about the deity of Christ.

5. Discuss why the Jews wanted to stone Jesus.

6. Talk about who receives eternal life, how long they keep it, and if anyone can take it away. As you discuss these things, concentrate on the fact that no one can ever take us out of Christ's hand, and note that we hear His voice because we are His sheep.

Point out that those who are truly His sheep will live differently from those who do not belong to Him.

7. Discuss the themes of John 9 and 10.

8. Conclude your class time with an overview of INSIGHTS ON SHEEP, and note why God refers to us as sheep. Ask how knowing these things can help us in our daily walk with the Shepherd, the Lord Jesus Christ. Keep the discussion as practical and specific as possible.

Week 7

Tell the class members that their seven weeks of commitment to this course comes to an end with this lesson. However, encourage them to continue, because the best is yet to come! If they would like to learn more about what it means to be a disciple of the Lord Jesus Christ and to live for Him and eventually with Him, they need to commit to six more weeks of study. It's a commitment that they will never regret, for during the next six weeks they will learn how to live in the power, peace, and comfort of the Holy Spirit.

1. Draw a map of Israel on the board and mark the locations of the major cities. Review the locations of the major events your class has studied in John 1–10, moving through John chapter by chapter and reviewing what happened and where it occurred. Remember to leave enough time for your discussion of John 11.

Be certain to cover the following:

a. John 1—Bethany; baptism of Jesus at the Jordan River; Galilee

b. John 2—Wedding at Cana; Jesus went to Capernaum, then to Jerusalem

c. John 3—Nicodemus in Jerusalem

d. John 4—Jesus goes from Judea to Galilee through Samaria to minister to the Samaritan woman at the well

e. John 5—To Jerusalem for a feast of the Jews

f. John 6—To the Sea of Galilee, where He feeds the 5,000

g. John 7—Jesus leaves the Sea of Galilee, goes up to Jerusalem for the Feast of Booths

h. John 8—Jesus goes to the Mount of Olives, then to the Temple (in Jerusalem), where He talks with the Jews, telling them His testimony is true

i. John 9—Jesus goes out of the Temple and heals a man who was blind from birth

j. John 10—Jesus gives discourse on the sheep and the Shepherd in Jerusalem; Feast of Dedication; Jesus leaves to go beyond the Jordan to where John was first baptizing and stays there awhile

k. John 11—Jesus leaves to go to Judea and visits Bethany, the village of Mary, Martha, and Lazarus—two miles from Jerusalem

2. Ask the class what miraculous sign is performed in John 11. Why is it such an important sign? What does this sign show about Jesus?

3. List insights from John 11 under the following headings: **Lazarus, Mary, Martha**.

4. Now, ask the class the following questions:

a. Is God there?

b. Does He care?

c. Do you think He knows about you?

    d. Did He know about Lazarus? What did He know about Lazarus? Make sure the class sees that Jesus not only knew about Lazarus' sickness and his death, He also knew that Lazarus would be raised from the dead. (Mention that Jesus was deeply moved and troubled over the grief of His loved ones, and that the people noticed His love for Lazarus.)

5. Discuss the Jews' reaction to the signs Jesus was performing, including the resurrection of Lazarus from the dead. What did they want to do to Jesus? Ask what that shows about the hearts of these men.

6. John 11:54 is a key transition verse in the Gospel of John because it marks the end of Jesus' public ministry. Have the class look at the first segment division on the JOHN AT A GLANCE chart and note to whom Jesus is going to minister next—His disciples (followers, learners).

7. Discuss the theme of John 11.

8. Spend time in prayer. Worship God together by thanking Him for the various truths everyone has learned about Him thus far. Encourage each person to mention at least one thing they have learned about the Father, the Son, or the Holy Spirit, and ask everyone to share what has happened in their understanding and their lives as a result of the weekly studies. Then ask them to pray for one another.

Week 8

1. Move through John 12 paragraph by paragraph and record the essence of each paragraph on the board. Ask what these insights mean to the class personally. For example:

a. Ask what they learn about Mary's devotion to Jesus and the response of Judas. Ask how people might respond to our devotion to the Lord.

b. Talk about Jesus riding into Jerusalem on a donkey and being heralded as the King. Did Jesus tell the crowd that they were wrong? What does His response to this acclamation indicate? What does His being King mean to them and their relationship to Him?

c. When you come to the passage about "a grain of wheat," discuss the illustration and what it means personally to their life for Christ.

d. Discuss John 12:27-50 as one unit so you will have adequate time for John 13. In this last segment of John 12, discuss Jesus' purpose in coming to earth. Point out that through Jesus' death for our sins, Satan's power is broken and, therefore, the "ruler of this world will be cast out."

Read Ephesians 2:1-3, where we see Satan's power over our lives before we receive the Lord Jesus Christ. It's important to know Satan's power is broken, because some people live in great fear of Satan and his demons. They need to understand that God has not given us a spirit of timidity, but of power, love, and discipline—a mind that is under control (2 Timothy 1:7).

Also, discuss the contrast between light and darkness and what happens when we believe. Help your class see that to refuse Jesus' sayings is to reject Him. Make it clear to them that if they say they believe in Jesus, then they must also believe the Word of God.

2. Discuss what happened in John 13 as Jesus and His disciples celebrated the Passover.

a. Examine this passage very carefully by using the 5 W's and an H. Talk about all that Jesus did, including WHY

He washed the disciples' feet. WHAT does His example tell us about how we are to live? HOW can others tell we are Jesus' disciples?

b. Discuss Judas' betrayal of the Lord Jesus Christ. Have the class read John 2:24-25; 6:64. Can we hide things in our hearts from God? What does that truth mean to us personally? What should we do, then, when we are tempted to keep things in our hearts that shouldn't be there?

c. Examine Peter's promise to Jesus and Jesus' response.

3. Talk about the themes of John 12 and 13.

4. Finally, give the class an opportunity to share what meant the most to them in this week's lesson. Ask if they have any questions, if there is anything they want to share, or if there is anything they want the class to pray about.

Week 9

John 14 and 15 are awesome chapters! Get on your knees and ask the Holy Spirit to show you the most effective way to lead this class for your particular group. I'll give you some suggestions, but let God lead you. Just be sure to cover the content of these chapters. The Holy Spirit will show you where the emphasis needs to be for your group.

1. Write three column headings on the board: **The Father, The Son, The Holy Spirit**. Have the class share everything they learned from John 14 and 15 about each person of the Godhead, and list their observations in the appropriate columns.

a. Since this is the first time in the Gospel of John that you have so much information about the Holy Spirit, you will want to be sure to use the 5 W's and an H. Note WHO the Spirit is, HOW He is described, WHAT He does, WHAT He is called, WHERE He is, and HOW the world responds to Him when He comes.

b. As you look at each person of the Godhead, note what each One gives or promises.

c. After you observe and discuss each person of the God-head, then talk about what these truths mean to the people in your class personally. How could knowing these truths affect their lives or change the way they live?

2. Have the class read John 15:16 aloud. Emphasize the fact that *God* has chosen them. What a comfort, honor, blessing, and privilege! At this point you might want to have the class thank God for this wonderful truth and for the promise that whatever we ask in His name (according to His character and purpose), He will do. Awesome!

3. Compare John 15:7 with 15:6. Mention how important it is for His words to abide (be at home) in us and for us to abide in them. Point out that this is the reason it's important for us to study the Bible regularly.

4. Write three headings on the board: **The Vine, The Vine-dresser, The Branches.** Review what the class discovered in the allegory of the vine and the branches. List the points they share.

Discuss what it means to abide in Jesus, and apply this informa-tion to the 11 disciples and Judas. Judas would soon betray Jesus. Discuss, too, the fact that Peter would deny Jesus but not betray Him, and that he would return to serve the Lord and eventually die for Him. Peter's death is predicted by Jesus in John 21, which we will study during our last week together.

5. Ask the class to discuss the themes of John 14 and 15.

6. Once again, give the class an opportunity to share what is happening to them personally as they do these weekly studies. If the Lord leads you to do so, give them an opportunity to pray and tell God that they believe on the Lord Jesus Christ, want to follow Him as His disciple, and want to have the Holy Spirit live within them as their comforter, helper, and guide.

Special note: Because next week's discussion will build on what you studied this week, you should save all the class observations on **The Father, The Son, The Holy Spirit**. Put this information back on the board before next week's discussion begins. Then when the class shares what they learned about each person of the Trinity in John 16, you will have a comprehensive list that includes both John 15 and 16.

Week 10

Before your group arrives, write on the board the insights that were shared last week under the headings **The Father, The Son, The Holy Spirit**.

1. Discuss and list on the board insights gained from John 16 about the Father, Son, and Holy Spirit.

2. Next, ask the group to go back through John 1–14 and share any additional insights they gained on the Holy Spirit. Add these to the list on the board.

3. Ask the class what they learned from John 14–16 about those who come to the Father through the Son. In your discussion, be sure to talk about the cost of following Jesus. Ask how the world will respond to those who follow Jesus, according to John 15:17-25. Talk also about how Jesus prepared His disciples for tribulation in John 16. Talk about the importance of loving one another.

4. How do the things the class just talked about in step three apply to daily life? Be sure the applications are practical.

5. Talk about the theme of John 16.

6. Encourage your students to talk about the tribulation they might face, have faced, or are dealing with right now. Have them discuss their fears as well as victories, and then pray for one another. Remember, dear leader, that love is key. Ask God to fill you with love for your students—a love that is more than words.

Week 11

As you study John 17 this week, remind your students that this prayer reveals God's heart for them. (Have everyone zero in on verse 20 so they see that John is for them as well as the disciples.) As you lead this discussion, have the group share how this prayer affirms that God is there, that He does care, and that He does know about them.

1. List on the board any insights the class shares regarding the prayer for the 11 disciples and for all future people who would believe in Jesus through their word.

2. Discuss Jesus' example and how the class can model it in their own lives. Since reading Jesus' prayer for His loved ones means so much to us, suggest that everyone consider writing out a prayer for their loved ones. They may not want to show what they wrote, but it could be a wonderful legacy!

3. What did the group learn from John 17 about the importance of the Word of God? Ask what they think the evil one's (Satan's) connection is with the world. What is their assurance in this chapter in relation to the evil one? What is their responsibility? Ask the class members if they are careful about their associations with others as well as what they watch, hear, listen to, and believe. Assure them that if they will stay in God's Word and determine in their hearts to obey it, they will have nothing to fear from the world nor the evil one.

4. Be sure to ask about the theme of John 17.

Week 12

Begin in prayer and ask the Holy Spirit to give each of you a glimpse of the great depth of God's love for you. Also, ask Him to show everyone what Jesus Christ endured in order to pay for their sins and for the sins of all mankind.

1. John 18 and 19 are two precious chapters that tell of our Lord's arrest, trial, and crucifixion. Go through the chapters paragraph by paragraph. Discuss what happens in each paragraph, and list these insights on the board.

2. Ask the group to think about the various people who met Jesus. Talk about how they interacted with Him and how He responded. Ask the students what they are learning about Jesus, people, and how to respond to others.

3. Discuss what the class learned by marking *sin, truth, King,* and *kingdom.*

4. Discuss the themes of John 18 and 19.

5. Close the discussion with a time of prayer. Urge each person to thank God for one truth they especially appreciated in John 18 or 19. Tell them that if they want to receive the Lord Jesus Christ as their Savior, they can pray to God and tell Him that they believe and that they want to be His child and live with Him forever. Those who already know Him may want to pray and affirm their commitment to continue pursuing holiness so their lives will be pleasing to Him.

Week 13

The bodily resurrection of our Lord Jesus Christ is an essential part of the gospel—the good news of salvation through faith in Jesus Christ. This reality is unique to Christianity. No other religion has a Savior who became like His followers, died for their sins, and then rose from the dead promising forgiveness of sins and eternal life to those who would believe. Because the resurrection is the corner-stone of our faith, be sure to let the class have adequate time to share all the facts about Jesus' resurrection.

Before you begin, write two headings on the board: **John 20** and **1 Corinthians 15**.

1. Examine what you learn in John 20 by using the 5 W's and an H and record all the facts on the board under the appropriate heading. Also, ask the class how John 21 shows proof of the resurrection.

2. Have the class read 1 Corinthians 15:1-8 on page 142 and point out the truths they learned about the resurrection. Put the facts under the appropriate heading.

3. Draw lines to connect the truths listed under **John 20** that parallel the truths listed under **1 Corinthians 15**.

4. How can the class know the resurrection is a sign? Compare this sign with the sign in John 11. What makes Jesus' resurrection a greater sign than that of Lazarus being raised from the dead? Did Jesus ever die again? No, but Lazarus would.

a. Have the group look up John 5:24 and John 6:39-40 and read them aloud. What is the promise for us who believe?

b. What about those who do not believe? Have the students read John 3:36. Those who do not believe are twice dead. They lived once but it was a life of death because they were dead in their trespasses and sins. They believed the father of lies, the devil, who is a murderer, instead of believing the One who laid down His life for them. So, they are twice dead. How sad!

5. Now, take your class to that wonderful final chapter of John and discuss what events took place.

6. List on the board what the class learned about Jesus, Peter, Jesus' sheep, and John.

> a. As you discuss Peter, note carefully how Jesus treated Peter. He didn't reject Peter, but called him to take care of His sheep.
>
> b. Note Peter's concern about John and how Jesus responded to Peter. Should we be concerned about what happens to other Christians and compare ourselves to them? No, we are to follow Jesus Christ unto death. Ask the class how committed they are to following Jesus.

Assure the students that no man can take their lives from them. They cannot die until the Lord Jesus Christ is ready to take them home. Discuss what they learned in this lesson about those who die as Christians.

7. Talk about the themes of John 20 and 21.

8. Ask the class how they are going to live in light of the truths they learned from John 20–21 as well as from the whole book of John.

9. Finally, close with a sweet time of prayer. Let everyone know how much you appreciate their faithfulness in finishing this course. If there are some who have not yet believed, continue to pray for them, for only God can save them. Remember, Jesus doesn't lose any of His sheep.

Blessings to you, precious child of God, for leading this study. Ask God what He wants you to do next. Remember, you are His workmanship created in Christ Jesus for good works that He has prepared beforehand for you to walk in (Ephesians 2:10). No matter what anyone else does, Beloved, keep following Him…and Him alone.

HARVEST HOUSE BOOKS BY KAY ARTHUR

~~~~~~~~

Discover the Bible for Yourself
God, Are You There?
God, Help Me Experience More of You
God, How Can I Live?
How to Study Your Bible
Israel, My Beloved
Just a Moment with You, God
Lord, Teach Me to Pray in 28 Days
Lord, Teach Me to Study the Bible in 28 Days
A Marriage Without Regrets
A Marriage Without Regrets Study Guide
Speak to My Heart, God
With an Everlasting Love
Youniquely Woman (with Emilie Barnes and Donna Otto)

~~~~~~~~

Bibles
The New Inductive Study Bible (NASB)

~~~~~~~~

Discover 4 Yourself® Inductive Bible Studies for Kids
God, What's Your Name?
How to Study Your Bible for Kids
Lord, Teach Me to Pray for Kids
God's Amazing Creation (Genesis 1–2)
Digging Up the Past (Genesis 3–11)
Abraham—God's Brave Explorer (Genesis 11–25)
Extreme Adventures with God (Isaac, Esau, and Jacob)
Joseph—God's Superhero (Genesis 37–50)
You're a Brave Man, Daniel! (Daniel 1–6)
Fast-Forward to the Future (Daniel 7–12)
Wrong Way, Jonah! (Jonah)
Jesus in the Spotlight (John 1–11)
Jesus—Awesome Power, Awesome Love (John 11–16)
Jesus—To Eternity and Beyond! (John 17–21)
Boy, Have I Got Problems! (James)
Bible Prophecy for Kids (Revelation 1–7)
A Sneak Peek into the Future (Revelation 8–22)